#8-12 BK Bnd June 2012

D1710521

COMPACT *Research*

Online
Social
Networking

Current Issues

ReferencePoint Press®

San Diego, CA

Select* books in the Compact Research series include:

Current Issues

Abortion
Animal Experimentation
Conflict in the Middle East
DNA Evidence and
    Investigation
Drugs and Sports
Gangs
Genetic Testing
Gun Control
Immigration

Islam
National Security
Nuclear Weapons and
    Security
Obesity
Stem Cells
Teen Smoking
Terrorist Attacks
Video Games

Diseases and Disorders

ADHD
Anorexia
Autism
Bipolar Disorders
Drug Addiction
HPV
Influenza
Mood Disorders

Obsessive-Compulsive
    Disorder
Phobias
Post-Traumatic Stress
    Disorder
Self-Injury Disorder
Sexually Transmitted
    Diseases

Drugs

Antidepressants
Club Drugs
Cocaine and Crack
Hallucinogens
Heroin
Inhalants
Marijuana

Methamphetamine
Nicotine and Tobacco
Painkillers
Performance-Enhancing
    Drugs
Prescription Drugs
Steroids

Energy and the Environment

Biofuels
Coal Power
Deforestation
Energy Alternatives
Garbage and Recycling
Global Warming and
    Climate Change

Hydrogen Power
Nuclear Power
Solar Power
Toxic Waste
Wind Power
World Energy Crisis

*For a complete list of titles please visit www.referencepointpress.com.

HM
742
.P37
2011

Online
Social
Networking

Peggy J. Parks

Current Issues

ReferencePoint
Press®

San Diego, CA

© 2011 ReferencePoint Press, Inc.

For more information, contact:
ReferencePoint Press, Inc.
PO Box 27779
San Diego, CA 92198
www.ReferencePointPress.com

Picture credits:
Cover: Dreamstime and iStockphoto.com
Maury Aaseng: 33–35, 47–49, 61–62, 75–77
AP Images: 15, 18

LIBRARY OF CONGRESS CATALOGING-IN-PUBLICATION DATA

Parks, Peggy J., 1951–
    Online social networking / by Peggy J. Parks.
        p. cm. — (Compact research series)
    ISBN-13: 978-1-60152-116-3 (hardback)
    ISBN-10: 1-60152-116-2 (hardback)
    1. Online social networks. 2. Internet—Social aspects. I. Title.
    HM742.P37   2011
    006.7'54—dc22
                                                                2010021701

Contents

Foreword

"Where is the knowledge we have lost in information?"

—T.S. Eliot, "The Rock."

As modern civilization continues to evolve, its ability to create, store, distribute, and access information expands exponentially. The explosion of information from all media continues to increase at a phenomenal rate. By 2020 some experts predict the worldwide information base will double every 73 days. While access to diverse sources of information and perspectives is paramount to any democratic society, information alone cannot help people gain knowledge and understanding. Information must be organized and presented clearly and succinctly in order to be understood. The challenge in the digital age becomes not the creation of information, but how best to sort, organize, enhance, and present information.

ReferencePoint Press developed the *Compact Research* series with this challenge of the information age in mind. More than any other subject area today, researching current issues can yield vast, diverse, and unqualified information that can be intimidating and overwhelming for even the most advanced and motivated researcher. The *Compact Research* series offers a compact, relevant, intelligent, and conveniently organized collection of information covering a variety of current topics ranging from illegal immigration and deforestation to diseases such as anorexia and meningitis.

The series focuses on three types of information: objective single-author narratives, opinion-based primary source quotations, and facts and statistics. The clearly written objective narratives provide context and reliable background information. Primary source quotes are carefully selected and cited, exposing the reader to differing points of view. And facts and statistics sections aid the reader in evaluating perspectives. Presenting these key types of information creates a richer, more balanced learning experience.

For better understanding and convenience, the series enhances information by organizing it into narrower topics and adding design features that make it easy for a reader to identify desired content. For example, in *Compact Research: Illegal Immigration*, a chapter covering the economic impact of illegal immigration has an objective narrative explaining the various ways the economy is impacted, a balanced section of numerous primary source quotes on the topic, followed by facts and full-color illustrations to encourage evaluation of contrasting perspectives.

The ancient Roman philosopher Lucius Annaeus Seneca wrote, "It is quality rather than quantity that matters." More than just a collection of content, the *Compact Research* series is simply committed to creating, finding, organizing, and presenting the most relevant and appropriate amount of information on a current topic in a user-friendly style that invites, intrigues, and fosters understanding.

Online Social Networking at a Glance

Online Social Networking Defined

Online social networking refers to interactive Web sites where people can post profiles, accumulate online friends, peruse their friends' friend lists, post photographs and videos, and communicate with each other.

Top Sites

As of March 2010 the five most popular social networking sites were Facebook, MySpace, Twitter, LinkedIn, and Classmates.

Phenomenal Growth

Facebook's growth has outpaced all other social networking sites, rising from 20 million U.S. users in 2007 to more than 103 million U.S. users in January 2010.

Typical Users

Adult Internet users between the ages of 18 and 24 frequent social networking sites more than any other age group, followed closely by teenage Internet users between the ages of 12 and 17.

Privacy Issues

Social networking sites have been criticized for not protecting users' personal information, leading to a May 2010 complaint filed with the Federal Trade Commission by 15 consumer advocacy groups.

Threats and Dangers

Identity theft, cyberbullying, online predators, and recruitment by terrorists are among the hazards of online social networking sites.

Sexting

Sexting is the sharing of sexually explicit photos or videos through social networking sites, e-mail, or cell phones, and it can have disastrous consequences.

Potential for Addiction

Whether online social networking can become addictive is controversial, although some mental health professionals say that tens of millions of people worldwide are addicted.

Regulation Issues

Tighter regulation of online social networking might help curtail cybercrime, Internet predators, and cyberbullying, but it might also erode the constitutional right to freedom of speech.

Overview

“**For many people, social networking has become as much of a daily routine as brewing coffee and brushing teeth.**”

—Bill Brenner, senior editor of *CSO* magazine, which provides news, analysis, and research on information technology and security issues.

“**Social network sites, online games, video-sharing sites, and gadgets such as iPods and mobile phones are now fixtures of youth culture. They have so permeated young lives that it is hard to believe that less than a decade ago these technologies barely existed.**”

—Mizuko Ito, a research scientist and lead author of the white paper *Living and Learning with New Media: Summary of Findings from the Digital Youth Project.*

Like all teenagers, Vivien had a deep desire to make friends, but getting to know people was not easy for her. Along with being a little shy, she believed that many of her classmates chose their friends based on having qualities that she lacked. "I'm not a cheerleader," she says. "I'm not the president of the student body. Or captain of the debate team. I'm not the prettiest girl in my class. I'm not the most popular girl in my class. I'm just a kid."[1]

Online social networking offered Vivien a venue in which her shyness was not a factor, and where she could talk freely about herself. Her hope was that people would see the things she posted on her Xanga site and like it so much that they would want to get to know her. She explains: "I go on these really great vacations with my parents between

10

Christmas and New Year's every year. And I take pictures of places we go. And I write about those places. And I post this on my Xanga. Because I think if kids in school read what I have to say and how I say it, they'll want to be my friend."[2]

How Does Online Social Networking Affect Human Interaction?

The term *social networking* has been around for years, since long before the Internet even existed. In general, it refers to individuals participating in specific groups based on common interests, such as sports teams, clubs, or community service groups. Online social networking is much the same, with people choosing sites based on their interests and the features that are offered. The popularity of these sites is growing at a rapid pace, as the Web site Social Networking explains:

> Although social networking is possible in person, especially in the workplace, universities, and high schools, it is most popular online. This is because unlike most high schools, colleges, or workplaces, the internet is filled with millions of individuals who are looking to meet other people, to gather and share first-hand information and experiences about any number of topics . . . from golfing, gardening, developing friendships and professional alliances.[3]

As social networking sites continue to grow more popular, and users spend increasing amounts of time online, some experts warn that this is leading to people becoming isolated from each other. This is the perspective of Aric Sigman, a British psychologist and author of the February 2009 report *Well Connected? The Biological Implications of "Social Networking."* Sigman cites studies of British citizens that show a correlation between greater use of the Internet and a decline in communication among family members and friends. This has led to depression and loneliness for those who

> " The term *social networking* has been around for years, since long before the Internet even existed.

have isolated themselves from real-life interaction, as Sigman writes: "They went on to report 'both social disengagement and worsening of mood . . . and limited face-to-face social interaction . . . poor quality of life and diminished physical and psychological health.'"[4]

An Evolving Internet

Although social networking sites are commonplace today, they are a relatively recent phenomenon whose existence would not be possible without the World Wide Web. Before the Web existed, the Internet was a complicated entity that only the savviest computer experts were able to navigate. A British technology whiz and computer consultant named Tim Berners-Lee wanted to change that, so he developed special software and the world's first point-and-click browser—and in doing so, he changed the nature of the Internet forever. In 1991, after Berners-Lee introduced his creation to technology professionals, the news raced throughout the Internet, and Web sites began to appear online. In 1993, 130 Web sites had been launched, and just 3 years later the number had grown to 100,000. By 1998 total sites had surpassed 2.5 million, and there appeared to be no end to the Web's extraordinary growth.

The soaring popularity of the Web ushered in a new phase of Internet activity: online social networking. One of the first of the online social networking sites, Classmates.com, was launched in 1995. Users could seek out and communicate with friends and acquaintances from grade school, middle school, high school, college, and the U.S. military. In 1997 the first site specifically created for social networking went online with the launch of SixDegrees.com. It was unique because it combined three features on one site: the ability of users to create online profiles, post lists of their friends, and peruse their friends' lists of friends. Each of these features had existed in some form on previously developed

> " The social networking site Friendster was introduced in 2002. Because it offered features that had not been available on other sites, it became wildly popular in a short period of time. "

sites, but SixDegrees.com was the first to combine them.

The social networking site Friendster was introduced in 2002. Because it offered features that had not been available on other sites, it became wildly popular in a short period of time. As social media researcher danah boyd writes:

> Although a handful of sites predated it, Friendster popularized the features that define contemporary social network sites—profiles, public testimonials or comments, and publicly articulated, traversable lists of friends. Launched in 2002 as a newfangled dating site, Friendster quickly became popular amongst mid-twenty/thirty-something urban dwellers living in the United States. Although some used the site for its intended purpose of meeting potential partners, others engaged in a wide array of activities, ranging from tracking down high school mates to creating fictional profiles for entertainment purposes.[5]

Not long after Friendster went online, other social networking sites were launched, such as MySpace in 2003 and Facebook in 2004.

Numerous Choices, Widespread Appeal

Groups that track Internet trends estimate that more than 300 social networking sites can be found online, although the number changes as new ones are launched and others close down. According to the Web analysis group Compete.com, the 5 most popular sites at the end of 2009 were Facebook, with 350 million members; MySpace, with 130 million; Twitter, with 75 million; Flixster, with 63 million; and LinkedIn (a business-oriented networking site), with 53 million. A more recent ranking was prepared in March 2010 by Daniel Nations, a technology specialist and Web trends guide for About.com. Using unique visits (whereby each visitor to the site is counted only once) rather than total site traffic, Nations calculates that Facebook, MySpace, and Twitter still remain the top 3 social networking sites. LinkedIn has replaced Flixster as the fourth most popular site, and Classmates.com has moved up to the number-5 spot.

People of all ages participate in online social networking, but teenagers and young adults represent the greatest number of users. According to a Pew Research Center survey published in January 2009, 65 percent

> **Growing numbers of business professionals are tapping into online social networks, particularly LinkedIn, which is the largest of all business-focused sites.**

of teen Internet users aged 12 to 17 use social networking sites, as do 75 percent of 18- to 24-year-olds. This can be compared with 57 percent of adult Internet users aged 25 to 34, 30 percent aged 35 to 44, 19 percent aged 45 to 54, 10 percent aged 55 to 64, and just 7 percent who are over 65 years old. As the survey's authors state: "At its core, use of online social networks is still a phenomenon of the young."[6]

As social networking sites continue to add new features that appeal to wider audiences, these sites are rapidly attracting older people. According to a February 2009 posting on Inside Facebook, that site has been growing in popularity among users over the age of 45, with a 165 percent increase among men and women during a 4-month period. The fastest-growing Facebook segment is women over 55, whose participation in the site caused a 175 percent spike in membership between September 2008 and February 2009.

From Tweeting to Networking

Initially designed as sites where people could socialize with friends, and perhaps find romantic relationships, online social networks continue to diversify. Facebook and MySpace are still used by many to keep up with friends and chat about their activities, and people use Twitter to keep their followers apprised of what they are doing with brief postings known as "tweets." But in addition to a purely social focus, these sites are also used to raise public awareness about the importance of current issues. For example, advocacy groups such as Sierra Club, Greenpeace, and World Wildlife Fund use social networking sites to tell the public about their activities and to build support for their causes. Legislators and political candidates have discovered that social networking sites are good vehicles for widely and quickly publicizing their views without having to incur expensive advertising costs.

Growing numbers of business professionals are tapping into online

Americans today are texting and tweeting and friending on a regular basis as online social networking becomes a fixture of daily life. Members of one North Carolina church (pictured) use online social networking as a means for sharing religious experiences.

social networks, particularly LinkedIn, which is the largest of all business-focused sites. Profiles that are posted on LinkedIn are similar to resumes, with details about members' education and employment experience. Users can interact with existing contacts to seek out new career opportunities and potential partnerships. As How Stuff Works writer Dave Roos explains: "If it turns out that your best friend went to college with the guy who's hiring, that could give you a significant advantage over other applicants."[7] LinkedIn is also used by professional employment recruiters. By paying a fee they can access LinkedIn Corporate Service, which allows them to run targeted searches for members based on qualifications and experience.

What Dangers Are Associated with Online Social Networking?

Millions of people find Facebook, MySpace, and other social networking sites to be enjoyable and fun—yet there are also dangers. Many users post personal information such as hometown, school, and/or place of employment, and are often careless about their privacy settings, which are designed to keep certain details hidden from people who just happen to be perusing the site. As a result, whatever people display could be observed by those who frequent the sites with the sole intent of committing crimes. Cybercriminals often assume false identities in order to lure unsuspecting victims into "friending" them—and unfortunately, many users, especially teenagers, do so without hesitation. Security consultant James Arlen says this is the result of naïveté on the part of those who use online social networking sites. He explains: "At the end of the day, far too many people operate in a zone where they presume trust. There's an odd level of trust where you look at someone's profile and say 'I know this person,' but there's no real attempt at authentication."[8] The more users open up their social networking pages to people they do not know, the more vulnerable they are to being victims of cybercrime.

> " The appeal of online social networking is not lost on gangs—members are finding the sites useful for communicating with each other and re-cruiting new members. "

Another danger associated with online social networking is cyberterrorism. Law enforcement agencies, including the FBI, say that terrorist groups use these sites to actively promote their causes and recruit new members. As terrorism expert Gabriel Weimann writes: "Research shows that about 90 percent of terrorist activity on the Internet consists of using social networking tools, be they independent bulletin boards, Paltalk, or Yahoo! eGroups." Weimann adds that when terrorists use online social networking sites, it poses a unique problem for law enforcement: "These forums act as a virtual firewall to safeguard the identities of those who participate, and they offer surfers easy access to terrorist material, to ask questions, and even to contribute and aid Cyber jihad."[9]

Networked Gangs

The appeal of online social networking is not lost on gangs—members are finding the sites useful for communicating with each other and recruiting new members. In addition, gangs use social networking to display gang signs and colors, spar with rival gangs, sell drugs, and even brag about crimes they have committed. Gang activity is most prolific on MySpace, which has long been the favored site for gangs, but their presence is also becoming more widespread on Twitter and Facebook. One of the world's most violent gangs, Mara Salvatrucha (MS-13), has been tied to dozens of Facebook accounts, with at least one site brazenly displaying photographs of dead members of a rival gang. Alberto Torrico, a member of the California state assembly, believes the proliferation of gangs on social

> **Sexting refers to the sharing of sexually explicit photos and/or videos by cell phone or online, and according to a September 2009 survey, the practice is becoming more common among teenagers.**

networking sites is a growing threat. He explains: "Social networking is a great way to reach out to others, update them on activities, exchange information and support a cause. Unfortunately, gangs are using these tools to communicate, recruit, issue threats, traffic narcotics, promote violence and expand their criminal activities."[10]

Although the presence of gangs on social networking sites is a problem for law enforcement, it has also proved to be a benefit. The information that is posted on the sites often helps investigators identify gang members and learn more about their organizations. Dean Johnston, who is with the California Bureau of Narcotics Enforcement, says this is proving to be a benefit for keeping track of gang activity. He explains: "You find out about people you never would have known about before. You build this little tree of people." In one California case much of the information that agents gathered came from gang members' Facebook accounts, which helped lead to arrests. "Once you get into a Facebook group, it's relatively easy," says Johnston. "You have a rolling commentary."[11]

Meanness Behind a Screen

Bullying is certainly not a new concept; it has always been an unfortunate reality that some people bully others whom they perceive to be

John Halligan (pictured) believes his son Ryan (shown in Web page) killed himself at the age of 13 because of vicious online bullying. Halligan and others have fought for laws that crack down on cyberbullying.

weaker than themselves. This is the case with cyberbullies as well, but rather than face-to-face contact, they harass and intimidate their victims using cell phone text messaging, e-mail, and/or online social networking sites. Cyberbullying has become a serious problem, and it is growing worse. According to a December 2008 report by a national task force charged with investigating Internet safety, cyberbullying poses the biggest online threat for young people. The authors write: "It is difficult to pinpoint the exact prevalence of cyberbullying and online harassment, because the definitions themselves vary, but the research is clear that this risk is the most common risk minors face online."[12]

> Sites such as Facebook, MySpace, Twitter, LinkedIn, and others are immensely popular; they attract hundreds of millions of users worldwide every day.

Surveys have shown that numerous adolescents and teens have been victims of cyberbullying. One study by psychologists from the University of California–Los Angeles revealed that nearly 3 out of 4 teenagers had been bullied online at least once during a 12-month period. The researchers learned those who were victims of cyberbullying rarely told anyone about it; only 10 percent of the teens who participated in the study reported what happened to their parents, teachers, or other adults. When asked why they kept this to themselves, half of the teens said they "need to learn to deal with it,"[13] and nearly one-third said they did not tell because they were afraid their parents might restrict their Internet access.

Teens and Sexting

Sexting is a relatively new phenomenon, one that is exclusively a product of the Internet age. Sexting refers to the sharing of sexually explicit photos and/or videos by cell phone or online, and according to a September 2009 survey, the practice is becoming more common among teenagers. Of those who participated in the survey, over one-fourth said that they had engaged in some form of sexting, and 10 percent of those said they had shared nude pictures of themselves. This is a seriously risky practice, as people have no way of knowing where the pictures will end up, who will see them, and what the consequences might be.

In some instances sexting has led to serious legal problems, as 18-year-old Phillip Alpert of Orlando, Florida, learned the hard way. After having a fight with his 16-year-old girlfriend, Alpert e-mailed nude photos of her to dozens of her friends and family members. He was arrested and charged with distributing child pornography, and was later convicted and sentenced to 5 years of probation. In addition, Alpert's name was added to the state's registered sex offender list—where it will remain until he is 43 years old.

Is Online Social Networking Addictive?

Whether people can become addicted to online social networking, or to the Internet in general, is a controversial issue. Some believe that the notion of Internet addiction is a myth, while others argue that such addictions can and do happen. Kimberly Young, who is clinical director of the Center for Internet Addiction Recovery, estimates that 5 to 10 percent of Americans—15 to 30 million people—suffer from Internet addiction. She explains: "I've seen a lot of growth in the field of Internet addiction. More research and studies (are) trying to understand it better."[14]

Should Online Social Networks Be More Tightly Regulated?

Online social networking sites have measures in place to help keep their networks safe, and some have committed to tightening security even further. For instance, in January 2008 MySpace officials reached an agreement with the National Association of Attorneys General to increase protections for young people using the site. Software was enhanced to identify underage users more effectively, and default settings for teenage users were changed to private so their sites could no longer be viewed by adults they did not know. In addition, MySpace retained a contractor to be responsible for identifying and eliminating inappropriate images from the site, as well as updating a list of pornographic Web sites and severing links between them and MySpace. More recently, in April 2010 MySpace added technology designed to identify and delete profiles of registered sex offenders, which led to 90,000 profiles being removed.

Even though Facebook, MySpace, and other social networking sites have security measures in place, this does not ensure that users are safe.

As the Facebook Statement of Rights and Responsibilities reads: "We do our best to keep Facebook safe, but we cannot guarantee it."[15] This lack of safety assurance is why many people believe that online social networking should be subject to rigorous legislation, rather than site officials being allowed to develop and monitor their own security policies. This is a contentious issue, however, because laws that would dictate what can and cannot be posted online may violate the constitutional right to freedom of speech. The issue continues to be debated among legislators, law enforcement professionals, and others who are concerned about the proliferation of harassment and crime through social networking sites.

Looking Ahead

There is no doubt that online social networking is here to stay. Sites such as Facebook, MySpace, Twitter, LinkedIn, and others are immensely popular; they attract hundreds of millions of users worldwide every day. As the sites offer even more advanced features, they will continue to rise in popularity and attract greater numbers of users. With the growing proliferation of these sites, safety and security issues will undoubtedly become even more of a concern than they are today. Will this lead to tighter regulation of online social networking? Because it is a controversial issue, that question cannot be answered with any certainty.

How Does Online Social Networking Affect Human Interaction?

66When I ask teenagers why they joined MySpace, the answer is simple: 'Cuz that's where my friends are.' Their explanation of what they do on the site is much more vague: 'I don't know . . . I just hang out.'99

—danah boyd, a researcher at Microsoft Research and a fellow at Harvard's Berkman Center for Internet and Society.

66I believe that in the future, social networks will be like air. They will be anywhere and everywhere we need and want them to be.99

—Charlene Li, an industry analyst who specializes in social technologies, interactive media, and marketing.

In survey after survey, teenagers have expressed their enthusiasm for online social networking, and one of its biggest fans is Sara Samuel. A high school junior from New Jersey, Samuel says one of the many reasons sites such as Facebook are so popular is because of how easily kids can communicate with each other. She explains: "Important updates on gossip or homework assignments are only a few clicks away. Sign on, send a message, receive an answer, and sign off. Communication really has been simplified, and the adolescent population of today is certainly capable and willing to use technology to their advantage."[16]

Samuel also likes online social networking because she can talk to friends about certain issues without having to look them in the face. She writes:

> With Facebook, emails and text messages, conversations can be had without the awkward silences that would be inevitable in a face-to-face interaction. No one is going to blurt out an embarrassing response to a question asked without forethought; having to type a message—as opposed to having to verbally answer on the spot—means having the ability to think about what one is going to say.[17]

Another of Samuel's favorite aspects of Facebook is the ability to find out instantaneously almost anything she wants to know about someone who interests her. As she explains: "With only a few clicks, a wealth of information about a crush, new lab partner, or the new kid in school is available. Pictures, applications, status updates, and maybe even a cell phone number—all information that can be available through text messages, Facebook, and emails."[18]

How the Internet Is Changing Society

When technology specialists talk about online social networking, they often use the term *Web 2.0*, which is loosely defined as the second generation World Wide Web. Not so long ago, visiting Web sites was a static experience that did not offer interactivity, but online social networking has radically changed that. Now these sites draw users in and make them part of the experience. As Web trends specialist Daniel Nations explains: "There is no clear definition of Web 2.0, and like many concepts, it has taken on a life of its own. But one thing is clear: Web 2.0 marks a fundamental change in how we use the Internet."[19]

Nations adds that with the advent of online social networking, the Internet has become more social, collaborative, in-

> " When technology specialists talk about online social networking, they often use the term *Web 2.0*, which is loosely defined as the second generation World Wide Web. "

teractive, and responsive, and this change has had a profound effect on everyone who uses it. "Web 2.0 marks a change in us as a society as well as the Internet as a technology," he writes. "In the early days of the web, we used it as a tool. Today, we aren't just using the Internet as a tool—we are becoming part of it. What is Web 2.0? *It is the process of putting us into the web.*"[20]

The Internet has transformed the way people think, communicate, do business, and go about many of their daily activities. Nations writes:

> Not only are we increasing our usage of the Internet—from how much time we spend on it at home to how we are increasingly carrying around a version of it in our pocket—but we are changing the way we interact with it. This has led us to a social web where we aren't just getting information dumped to us from a computer, but we are reaching out to connect with other people to hear what they have to say on a subject.[21]

Conflicting Perspectives

Some are concerned that online social networking interferes with real-life relationships, causing people to become isolated from each other and rely too heavily on electronic communication. This was the focus of psychologist Aric Sigman's February 2009 report *Well Connected? The Biological Implications of "Social Networking."* In reference to British society, he notes that in the past decade or two, couples have begun spending less time together and more time at work or elsewhere. Another of Sigman's concerns is that the time parents spend with their children has dramatically declined. He is convinced that a major factor in what he

> "Lauren became despondent, thinking of her former healthy, active lifestyle as only a distant memory. Then she learned about Starbright World, a social networking site for seriously ill teenagers—and it totally changed her life."

calls a "disinclination for togetherness" is new technologies, which he sees as a significant contributor to growing social isolation. He writes: "Whether in or out of the home, more people of *all* ages in the UK are physically and socially disengaged from the people around them because they are wearing earphones, talking or texting on a mobile telephone, or using a laptop or Blackberry."[22]

Sigman's concern about the influence of electronic communication is shared by some other researchers—but not everyone agrees. According to Nancy Baym, an associate professor of communication studies at the University of Kansas–Lawrence, the fear that online social networking adversely affects relationships is a concept that is not supported by research. She explains: "There's not compelling evidence that spending time on social networking sites and expanding our social circles damages the close relationships we have. People think if you're hanging out on Facebook, you're not having quality face-to-face time. That is not supported."[23]

Those who share Baym's perspective say that because online social networking is so pervasive in today's society, people are spending as much or more time communicating online than they do offline. Barry Wellman, a sociologist from Toronto, Canada, who has been analyzing this trend, states: "Social networking sites have brought social networks into people's consciousness." A 2009 study coauthored by Wellman found that heavy Internet users have the most friends, offline as well as online. "The mythology we have is that people used to spend whole days hanging around community—like the bar at *Cheers*. They didn't. They stayed home. If we switch from television to social networking sites, it's a switch toward sociability—not away from it."[24]

According to a November 2008 study by researchers from the University of Southern California and the University of California–Berkeley,

> " According to a November 2008 study by researchers from the University of Southern California and the University of California–Berkeley, time spent on social networking sites actually enhances real-life friendships. "

time spent on social networking sites actually enhances real-life friendships. Over a three-year period, the team interviewed more than 800 teens and young adults and spent more than 5,000 hours observing the participants' online behavior. They concluded that young people use social networking sites to extend the friendships they already have from school, religious organizations, sports, and other activities. The authors write:

> They can be "always on," in constant contact with their friends through private communications like instant messaging or mobile phones, as well as in public ways through social network sites such as MySpace and Facebook. With these "friendship-driven" practices, youth are almost always associating with people they already know in their offline lives. The majority of youth use new media to "hang out" and extend existing friendships in these ways.[25]

A Light in the Darkness

For teenagers who suffer from a chronic illness, life can be terribly lonely. They feel isolated, as though no one understands the pain, fear, and uncertainty that they experience day after day. This was the case with a teenage girl named Lauren, who was diagnosed with a rare nervous system disease when she was 13 years old. Over the following year her health continued to deteriorate until she was paralyzed, able to move nothing but her right hand. Because she also had a severe allergy to light, she was confined to total darkness. Unable to feed herself, get dressed, go to school, or even leave her dark room, Lauren became despondent, thinking of her former healthy, active lifestyle as only a distant memory. Then she learned about Starbright World, a social networking site for seriously ill teenagers—and it totally changed her life.

Once Lauren discovered Starbright, it was as though a whole new world had opened up to her. She could interact with other teenagers who were also suffering from serious illnesses, and she knew they understood what she was going through. She made many new friends and reveled in the fellowship and support that she had been longing for. She writes: "In the darkness, with only one hand on the computer, I was able to communicate with others who understood what it was like to be sick. I talked to kids about what was going on in my life and about the kinds of things they were suffering from. . . . I developed amazing friendships and felt like I belonged to this elite club made up of the bravest people I knew."[26] When Lauren was 19, her health slowly began to improve. She regained movement in her legs and arms, could tolerate small amounts of light, and was able to get around in a wheelchair.

Even when she began attending physical therapy and her schedule got busier, Lauren still signed on to Starbright World every day. That was where her best friends were, the people she could always count on when she needed them, the people who had helped her through the darkest moments of her life. Now in her twenties, she is happy and healthy, living in Los Angeles and pursuing her dream of becoming a writer. She reflects on the past and shares what her involvement in the social networking site did for her:

> "Online social networking has changed how people use the Internet—but even more profound is how dramatically it has changed the Internet itself."

There were times when being in bed and in the darkness took its toll on my spirit, but no matter the challenges, no matter the heartache or frustration, *Starbright World* was always a light that shone through the pain and made its way to me. . . . *Starbright World* was an escape from the confines of that dark room to a place with life, laughter and friendships. It was the one place where everyone understood me and welcomed me for who I was, not for what disease I had. There, I was simply Lauren.[27]

A Lifesaving Connection

For years Matthew Burge knew that his father, John, suffered from serious kidney disease that was growing progressively worse. When the doctor finally said that nothing more could be done and John's only hope of surviving was a kidney transplant, Matthew was desperate to do something to help. Knowing the worldwide reach of social networking sites, he used his Facebook page to post a message about his dad needing a kidney donor. When he received no responses, he was so discouraged that he was ready to give up on the site altogether, but then he decided to try once again. On September 18, 2009, Matthew posted: "If anyone wants to donate a kidney, my dad could really use one."[28] Less than half an hour later he saw a comment beneath his post. The message was not from a distant stranger; it was from Matthew's real-life friend, Nick Etten, who lived in the same town. Until Etten spotted the post on Facebook, he had not been aware that John Burge was so sick. Once he found out, he offered to donate a kidney.

On December 17, 2009, after tests confirmed a blood type match, surgeons removed one of Etten's kidneys and implanted it into John Burge. The operation was considered a total success. Burge later said that he would likely still be waiting for a kidney if his son had not been actively involved with Facebook and posted his request for help.

Something for Everyone

Online social networking is wildly popular with people all over the world. No matter what they are seeking or what their interests or needs are, there are numerous sites online just for them. Social networking allows users to chat with old and new friends, keep up on the latest news and gossip, and exchange photos and videos, as well as reach out for support or post a worldwide plea for help. Some experts are concerned that Facebook, MySpace, and other social networking sites are interfering with real-life communication, causing people to become more isolated from each other. Many others disagree, saying that research does not support this view. No matter what one's perspective happens to be, online social networking has changed how people use the Internet—but even more profound is how dramatically it has changed the Internet itself.

How Does Online Social Networking Affect Human Interaction?

> " The rapid proliferation of electronic media is now making private space available in almost every sphere of the individual's life. Yet this is now the most significant contributing factor to society's growing physical estrangement. "

—Aric Sigman, "Well Connected? The Biological Implications of 'Social Networking,'" *Biologist*, February 2009. www.aricsigman.com.

Sigman is an associate fellow of the British Psychological Society, a fellow of the Society of Biology, and the author of the book *The Spoilt Generation*.

> " Some doom-mongers have suggested that social networking technologies will eventually lead to a society in which we no longer engage in face-to-face contact with people. I don't see it. "

—William Reader, in Stephen J. Dubner, "Is MySpace Good for Society? A Freakonomics Quorum," *New York Times* Freakonomics blog, February 15, 2008. http://freakonomics.blogs.nytimes.com.

Reader is a professor of psychology at Sheffield Hallam University and a social networking site researcher.

Bracketed quotes indicate conflicting positions.

* Editor's Note: While the definition of a primary source can be narrowly or broadly defined, for the purposes of Compact Research, a primary source consists of: 1) results of original research presented by an organization or researcher; 2) eyewitness accounts of events, personal experience, or work experience; 3) first-person editorials offering pundits' opinions; 4) government officials presenting political plans and/or policies; 5) representatives of organizations presenting testimony or policy.

> **❝The growth in popularity of social networks—and the resultant broadening audience—is only half the story. The staggering increase in the amount of time people are spending on these sites is changing the way people spend their time online and has ramifications for how people behave, share and interact within their normal daily lives.❞**

—Nielsen Company, *Global Faces and Networked Places*, March 2009. http://blog.nielsen.com.

Nielsen is a marketing and media information company that is based in New York City.

> **❝I believe the benefits provided by social network sites such as Facebook have made us better off as a society and as individuals, and that, as they continue to be adopted by more diverse populations, we will see an increase in their utility.❞**

—Nicole Ellison, in Stephen J. Dubner, "Is MySpace Good for Society? A Freakonomics Quorum," *New York Times* Freakonomics blog, February 15, 2008. http://freakonomics.blogs.nytimes.com.

Ellison is an assistant professor of telecommunication, information studies, and media at Michigan State University.

> **❝We have entered a new age of excess. . . . We're turning toward an overabundance of blather, in the form of Insipid Status Update, over-posting of photos, over-liking of posts, and self-important drivel about what color socks we plan to wear and what brand of ketchup we prefer on our fries.❞**

—Janelle Randazza, *Go Tweet Yourself.* Avon, MA: Adams, 2009.

Randazza is a journalist and author who lives in Los Angeles.

> **❝Social networking services, such as Facebook, provide new opportunities for users to maintain core social networks. Core ties can be highly influential in decision making and exposure to ideas, issues and opinion.❞**

—Pew Research Center, *Social Isolation and New Technology*, November 4, 2009. http://pewresearch.org.

The Pew Research Center provides information on issues, attitudes, and trends shaping America and the world.

66 Thanks to their viral nature, we have reached the tipping point in the mass adoption of online social networks, and they will only continue growing in prominence and pervasiveness. One would be hard-pressed to find a high school or college student today who doesn't use Facebook or MySpace. **99**

Clara Shih, *The Facebook Era*. Boston: Prentice Hall, 2009.

Shih is a technology and Internet specialist who has worked for Microsoft, Google, and Facebook.

66 Technology affords young people many benefits: the ability to talk to people worldwide, to more easily and regularly communicate with family and peers, and to make rewarding social connections that may be difficult to make in person. Some young people report that they feel better about themselves on-line than they do in the real world and feel it is easier to be accepted on-line. **99**

—Corinne David-Ferdon and Marci Feldman Hertz, *Electronic Media and Youth Violence: A CDC Issue Brief for Researchers*, 2009. www.cdc.gov.

David-Ferdon and Hertz are with the Centers for Disease Control and Prevention.

66 Many people using Facebook are discarding all forms of social etiquette. While some offer warm messages, others zing insults. They broadcast everything about their lives I have no desire or business knowing. **99**

—Yvonne Fournier, "Facebook Dangers: Parents Cannot Patrol the Social Networking World," July 1, 2009. http://newsblaze.com.

Fournier is a former pharmacist and public health administrator who is now an educator and child advocate.

66 The key is that as you're getting known online, the Internet is one big networking party. Just because you can hide behind your monitor doesn't mean that you're invisible. **99**

—Penny C. Sansevieri, "Social Networking on Blogs," *Huffington Post*, December 31, 2009. www.huffingtonpost.com.

Sansevieri is the founder of Author Marketing Experts, a marketing and public relations firm based in San Diego.

Facts and Illustrations

How Does Online Social Networking Affect Human Interaction?

- A poll released in August 2009 by Common Sense Media showed that **22 percent** of teenagers check social networking sites more than 10 times a day, while only **4 percent** of parents believe their kids are checking the sites that often.

- A study published in November 2009 by the University of Michigan's C.S. Mott Children's Hospital showed that for kids using the Internet, **66 percent** of teens aged 13 to 17 have their own social networking profiles, as do **19 percent** of preteens aged 9 to 12.

- In response to a survey published in April 2009 by the Center for the Digital Future, **87 percent** of adults said that the children in their household spend the same amount of time or more time with friends since using the Internet.

- A Pew Research Center survey published in January 2009 showed that **75 percent** of Internet users aged 18 to 24 had a profile on a social network site, compared with **57 percent** of those aged 25 to 34.

- According to a May 2010 CNN report, Twitter users create **50 million** tweets each day.

- Researchers from the University of Georgia studied the correlation between **narcissism (excessive self-love)** and Facebook usage and reported in September 2008 that the more "friends" and wall posts users had, the more narcissistic they were.

Facebook Is the Top Social Networking Site

Millions of people throughout the world are active in online social networking and the popularity of these sites has soared in recent years—with Facebook the leader by a huge margin. This shows the top four.

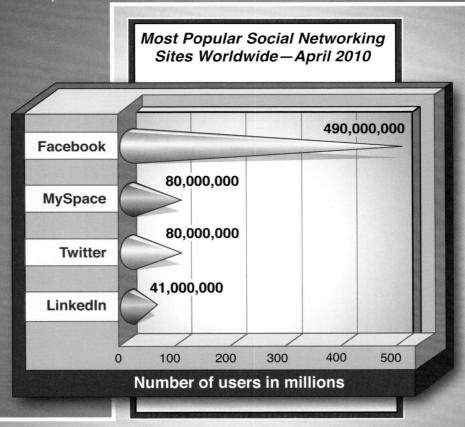

Most Popular Social Networking Sites Worldwide—April 2010

Site	Number of users in millions
Facebook	490,000,000
MySpace	80,000,000
Twitter	80,000,000
LinkedIn	41,000,000

Number of users in millions

Source: Paul Kiser, "Who Uses Facebook, MySpace, Twitter, and LinkedIn?" Paul Kiser's Blog, April 1, 2010. http://paulkiser.wordpress.com.

- A survey published in 2009 by the Pew Research Center showed that teenagers and young adults aged 18 to 32 were the most likely group to use the Internet for entertainment and for **communicating with friends and family**.

Teens Prefer Texting

In a survey conducted by Pew Research Center between June and October 2009, 800 teenagers shared information about how they typically communicate with their friends. Respondents in all age groups prefer cell phone texting over social networking sites.

Percent of teens who contact their friends daily by text messaging and/or social networking sites

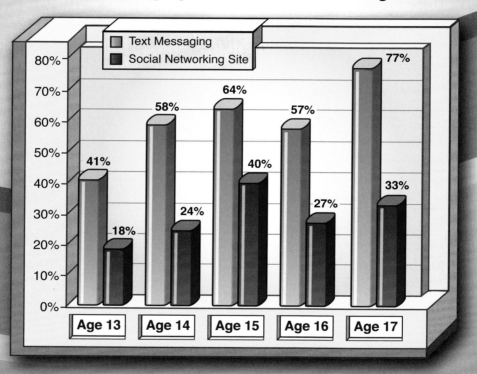

Source: Pew Research Center, "Teens, Cell Phones and Texting," Pew Internet & American Life Project, April 20, 2010. http://pewresearch.org.

- A study released in February 2010 by the public relations firm Ruder Finn states that **91 percent** of mobile phone users go online to access social networking sites, compared with **79 percent** of traditional desktop computer users.

Facebook Users in the United States

Since Facebook was launched in 2004 its growth has been phenomenal, and today it far outranks all other social networking sites. This table shows the growth rates of Facebook's various user bases* from January 4, 2009, to January 4, 2010.

Gender	As of 1/04/2009		As of 1/04/2010		
	Users	Percentage	Users	Percentage	Growth
Males	17,747,880	42.2%	43,932,140	42.6%	147.5%
Females	23,429,960	55.7%	56,026,560	54.3%	139.1%
Unknown	911,360	2.2%	3,126,820	3.03%	243.1%
Total US	42,089,200	100.0%	103,085,520	100.0%	144.9%
Age					
13–17	5,674,780	13.5%	10,680,140	10.4%	88.2%
18–24	17,192,360	40.8%	26,075,960	25.3%	51.7%
25–34	11,254,700	26.7%	25,580,100	24.8%	127.3%
35–54	6,989,200	16.6%	29,917,640	29.0%	328.1%
55+	954,680	2.3%	9,763,900	9.5%	922.7%
Unknown	23,480	0.1%	1,067,780	1.0%	4447.6%
Current Enrollment					
High School	5,627,740	13.4%	7,989,620	7.8%	42.0%
College	7,833,280	18.6%	3,521,900	3.4%	-55.0%
Alumni	4,756,480	11.3%	32,350,260	31.4%	580.1%
Unknown	23,871,700	56.7%	59,223,740	57.5%	148.1%

*Refers to U.S. users only.

Source: Peter Corbett, "Facebook Demographics and Statistics Report 2010—145% Growth in 1 Year," iStrategy Labs, January 4, 2010. www.istrategylabs.com.

What Dangers Are Associated with Online Social Networking?

66'A place for friends.' Well I can tell you I've found a fair number of enemies on MySpace too. How about 'A place for friends, enemies, freaks, and pornographers?' That might be more accurate.99

—Janelle Randazza, a journalist and author of the book *Go Tweet Yourself.*

66Unfortunately, those who do not understand social media look to the news, see the negative coverage, and declare all social media evil.99

—danah boyd, a researcher at Microsoft Research and a fellow at Harvard's Berkman Center for Internet and Society.

When 18-year-old Caitlin Davis decided to audition for the New England Patriots cheerleading squad, she knew she would face tough competition. Out of 300 young women trying out, including veteran cheerleaders who were reauditioning, only 23 would be chosen. On April 5, 2008, when the winners were announced, Davis was thrilled to be one of them—and she had no way of knowing that her stint as a Patriots cheerleader would come to an abrupt end just 7 months later. After pictures taken at a Halloween party were posted on Facebook, Davis was promptly kicked off the squad.

The party was held in a dorm at Boston College, and Davis attended with some of her friends. The photos show her smiling at the camera and holding a Sharpie marker as she kneels next to a young man who was drunk and passed out. The entire upper half of his body, including his face, was covered in vulgar drawings and words; the phrase "I am a Jew;" and swastikas, the symbols used by the Nazi party. After the photographs surfaced on Facebook, they were picked up by the Web site On Blast at Last, and from there they raced throughout the Internet. Although Davis denied drawing on the unconscious man, saying that his friends had done it as a Halloween prank, being captured on camera with a marker in her hand suggested otherwise.

As soon as Patriots officials became aware of the photographs, they fired Davis and announced that she was no longer a member of the squad. A commentator for Yahoo! Sports shares his thoughts about the damage that can be done by what is posted on social networking sites:

> The whole incident highlights maybe my least favorite parts of the internet. First, the entire Facebook and MySpace phenomenon, where people have an absolutely bizarre urge to share the most intimate details of their personal lives on the web for anyone to see. I absolutely do not get that. I love the idea that the internet connects us all, and lets us share ideas and thoughts and everything else, but I don't understand the need, which a lot of people have, to post everything about yourself on Facebook and say, "Here I am, world! Here's me in a variety of compromising positions! Enjoy!" And I hate how that leads to the whole "GOTCHA!" phenomenon that the internet is so fond of these days, in which a website like [On Blast at Last] can stumble upon these pictures, and then use them to take apart your life.[29]

Shrewd Cybercriminals

Online social networks are extremely popular, which is why they have experienced phenomenal growth in recent years. These sites have also given cybercriminals a whole new world of opportunity. As the *Security Threat Report: 2010* explains: "2009 saw Facebook, Twitter and other social networking sites solidify their position at the heart of many users' daily internet activities, and saw these websites become a primary target for hackers. Because of this, social networks have become one of the most significant vectors for data loss and identity theft."[30]

One reason social networking sites are so vulnerable is that hackers know how easily they can obtain information from users who are careless about what they post and whom they share it with. An article on the Go Banking Rates Web site states: "As you can imagine, identity thieves can be very savvy individuals. They know you're probably trying to protect your identity like many others, so they come up with tons of ways to convince you to give up your identity or part ways with your money."[31] By studying someone's friend list on sites such as Facebook or MySpace, a thief can gain enough information to create a false profile, and then lure the unsuspecting person into adding him or her as a friend.

> " One reason social networking sites are so vulnerable is that hackers know how easily they can obtain information from users who are careless about what they post and whom they share it with. "

Once this happens, the "friend" may claim to be in trouble and request that emergency money be wired, or even be so bold as to ask for credit card numbers. As Go Banking Rates explains: "You may assume that you wouldn't trust this person, but keep in mind that the thief has already gauged the activities of your friend who has given too much information about his or her life. Now all the thief has to do is mirror the conversations posted right on the walls to get important information from you."[32]

The Perils of Sexting

Although no one knows where the term *sexting* originated or when it was first used, the National Center for Missing and Exploited Children says it is a recent phenomenon: "Two years ago, the word 'sexting' did not even exist in the English language. Today it is a term that is much discussed and debated by parents, students, educators, law enforcement leaders and policy makers across America."[33] *Sexting* is a spinoff of the word *texting*. It originally referred to the sharing of sexually explicit or nude photographs via cell phone text messages, but now also includes social networking sites and e-mail. No matter what electronic medium is used, this is risky behavior that can result in disastrous consequences. Sexting has led to humiliation, ruined reputations, lost job opportunities, denial of college admissions, and a host of other problems as a result of lewd materials falling into the wrong hands.

In spite of the risks involved, studies have shown that sexting is not uncommon among teenagers. This became apparent during a survey released in 2009 that was conducted on behalf of the National Center for Missing and Exploited Children. It found that 19 percent of teens had sent, received, or forwarded sexually suggestive nude or nearly nude photos through text messages or e-mails. Of the teens who had participated in sexting, 60 percent had sent the photos to a boyfriend and/or girlfriend, and 11 percent had sent them to someone they did not know.

Relentless Online Harassment

Whether it involves physical abuse, taunting, name-calling, or the spread of rumors, bullying by classmates has long been an unfortunate fact of life for many young people. While enduring this can be extremely painful for victims, the bullying of the past generally stopped when school ended—but such is not the case with cyberbullying. Scott Hirschfeld, who is with the Anti-Defamation League's education division, explains: "With electronic forms of bullying there is no refuge. Here it is 24/7. It is always online. Even if you turn off your computer you know that web page is up, or that people are spreading this rumor about you. The relentlessness of it is very psychologically devastating."[34]

Cyberbullying has been identified as one of the most serious problems associated with online social networking, and numerous young people have been victims of it. A

> **Sexting has led to humiliation, ruined reputations, lost job opportunities, denial of college admissions, and a host of other problems as a result of lewd materials falling into the wrong hands.**

study published in 2008 by researchers at the University of California–Los Angeles (UCLA) showed that 41 percent of teenagers surveyed had experienced online bullying between 1 and 3 times over the course of a year, 13 percent reported 4 to 6 incidents, and 19 percent reported 7 or more incidents. A UCLA press release explains: "The most prevalent forms of bullying online and in school involved name-calling or insults. . . . Bullying also includes threats, sending embarrassing pictures, sharing private information without permission and spreading nasty rumors."[35]

> Cyberbullying has been identified as one of the most serious problems associated with online social networking, and numerous young people have been victims of it.

Jessica Logan endured relentless cyberbullying that ultimately resulted in her suicide. A pretty, bubbly, artistic teenager from Ohio, Logan had many friends and had been dating her boyfriend for several months. One day she took a nude photo of herself from the neck down and sent it to him from her cell phone, trusting that he would keep it to himself. But after they broke up, he sent the photo to four girls, who then forwarded it to others. Within a short period of time, hundreds of kids in Logan's high school and at least five other schools in the Cincinnati area had seen the photo—and that was when her nightmare began. Both in person and online, she was harassed, called vile names, and shunned.

The smear campaign against Logan continued, causing the once happy, vivacious teenager to become depressed and withdrawn. Her best friend, Lauren Taylor, explains: "She just totally changed. She wasn't as outgoing and kind of kept to herself, where she would normally be like jumping around. Instead her head was just down, and she would always be crying. I remember her constantly calling my phone crying."[36] Taylor says that there was no way for Logan to escape from the abuse—it followed her everywhere. Taylor explains:

> I'd be with her and she'd get numbers that weren't even in her contacts, random numbers that she didn't know,

texting her, "You're a whore, you're a slut." Or, she'd get on MySpace and get messages from people calling her those names, or Facebook would be the same way. It was constant. She'd go home thinking, "Oh I'm going to get away from this," but she never could get away from it.[37]

Finally, Logan decided to appear on a news program to talk about what happened to her. After suffering for so long, she wanted to tell her story in the hope that others might avoid the same fate. In May 2008 she was featured on the program with her image blurred and her voice distorted, and she wept as she told the commentator: "I still get harassed and stuff. I just want to make sure no one else will have to go through this same thing."[38] Even though Logan had appeared on the show anonymously, the students knew it was her, and the harassment worsened. On July 3, 2008, she went to the funeral of a close friend who had committed suicide—and that evening, filled with despair, Logan hanged herself in her bedroom.

Preying on the Young

According to a study in the February/March 2008 issue of *American Psychologist*, most Internet-related sex crimes result from men who befriend teenagers online, mostly 13- to 15-year-old girls, and gain their trust. Once a friendship has developed, the man attempts to seduce the teen, making it clear that he is interested in a sexual relationship, and the teen begins to feel an intimate bond with him. As researcher Janis Wolak writes: "From the perspective of the victim, these are romances."[39] The teen becomes eager to meet in person and make the virtual romance a real one—and this can lead to the kind of dangerous situation that cost Ashleigh Hall her life.

> As popular as social networking sites are, and as much as people enjoy them, there is a dark side as well.

Hall, a 17-year-old girl from England, developed a romantic attachment to someone she thought was a boy named Pete Cartwright. His Facebook profile showed photographs of a handsome young man in his late teens. The "teenage boy," however, was actually Peter Chapman, a 33-year-old convicted rapist who had created a fake online persona. Excited about her budding romance, Hall gave him her cell phone number, and they made a date to get together. "Pete" had told her that his father would pick her up and take her to meet him, so she had no hesitation about going with Chapman when he arrived.

Once he had Hall in the car, he drove to a deserted area, where he bound her wrists, mouth, and nose with duct tape, and then raped her. Unable to breathe, she slowly suffocated to death, and Chapman dumped her body in a ditch. Within hours, he was back online trying to arrange a date with one of the other young women he had deceived on Facebook. He was later arrested, convicted of kidnapping, rape, and murder, and sent to prison for life. After Chapman's sentencing, police detective Andy Reddick issued a warning for others: "It's clear from our investigation that sexual predators are using these sites to target their next victim. Our message today is do not meet people who you have only met on social networking sites."[40]

Real Dangers, Serious Threats

As popular as social networking sites are, and as much as people enjoy them, there is a dark side as well. Photographs posted online or shared via cell phone can come back to haunt someone later, resulting in a ruined reputation or the loss of a job. Cyberbullying can cause unbearable pain and suffering, even to the point that a victim believes life is no longer worth living. Online predators can trick young people to gain their trust, and then cause them harm or even kill them. These and other threats should not necessarily frighten people into avoiding online social networking altogether, but they should serve as a warning that the potential dangers should never be taken lightly.

What Dangers Are Associated with Online Social Networking?

> **Statistics already show that 1 in 5 children are approached by a cyber-predator making child Internet safety a number one parental priority.**

—Center for Internet Addiction Recovery, "For the Professional," August 24, 2009. www.netaddiction.com.

The Center for Internet Addiction Recovery is devoted to helping those who suffer from Internet addiction.

> **The publicity about online 'predators' who prey on naïve children using trickery and violence is largely inaccurate.**

—Janis Wolak, David Finkelhor, Kimberly J. Mitchell, and Michele L. Ybarra, "Online 'Predators' and Their Victims," *American Psychologist*, February–March 2008. www.apa.org.

Wolak, Finkelhor, and Mitchell are with the Crimes Against Children Research Center at the University of New Hampshire, and Ybarra is with Internet Solutions for Kids.

Bracketed quotes indicate conflicting positions.

* Editor's Note: While the definition of a primary source can be narrowly or broadly defined, for the purposes of Compact Research, a primary source consists of: 1) results of original research presented by an organization or researcher; 2) eyewitness accounts of events, personal experience, or work experience; 3) first-person editorials offering pundits' opinions; 4) government officials presenting political plans and/or policies; 5) representatives of organizations presenting testimony or policy.

❝By harnessing the power of a global community created by online social networks to their advantage, not only can terrorists promote global paranoia, share their messages with sympathizers and obtain donations; they can also create more terrorists.❞

—Gabriel Weimann, "Terrorism's New Avatars—Part II," *YaleGlobal Online*, January 12, 2010. http://yaleglobal.yale.edu.

Weimann is a professor of communications at Haifa University in Israel and the School of International Studies in Washington, D.C.

❝That person with the attractive profile picture who just friended you—and suddenly needs money—is probably some cybercriminal looking for easy cash. Think twice before acting.❞

—Symantec, "Top 5 Social Media Scams," *ClubNorton*, May 2010. www.symantec.com.

Symantec is one of the world's largest security software companies.

❝From bullying on the playground and hallways at school to 'cyber-bullying,' this crisis is reaching epidemic proportions.❞

—Wendy Miron, "Re: Bullies Beware!" letter to the editor, *Peshtigo Times*, 2010. www.peshtigotimes.net.

Miron is the codirector of Bully Police USA Wisconsin, North, a watchdog organization that advocates for young people who have been victims of bullying and reports on state antibullying laws.

❝The first things you need to know about cyberbullying are that it's not an epidemic and it's not killing our children.❞

—Larry Magid, "How to Stop Cyberbullying," SafeKids, July 14, 2009. www.safekids.com.

Magid is a technology journalist, Internet safety advocate, and the founder of the Web site SafeKids.

66Today, more and more people are using the Web for information, communication and entertainment. At the same time Internet users are abusing the Web to spread discriminatory rhetoric and to incite . . . hatred.**99**

—International Network Against Cyberhate, *Report 2009*, November 2009. www.inach.net.

The mission of the International Network Against Cyberhate is to promote respect, responsibility, and citizenship on the Internet through countering cyberhate and raising awareness about online discrimination.

66'Cyber-bullying' is a loaded term to be avoided by anyone interested in engaging in an objective look at online speech.**99**

—James Tucker, "Free Speech and 'Cyber-Bullying,'" American Civil Liberties Union Blog of Rights, January 16, 2008. www.aclu.org.

Tucker is a policy counsel with the American Civil Liberties Union.

66'Sexting' refers to sending a text message with pictures of children or teens that are inappropriate, naked or engaged in sex acts. . . . The emotional pain it causes can be enormous for the child in the picture as well as the sender and receiver—often with legal implications.**99**

—American Academy of Pediatrics, "Talking to Kids and Teens About Social Media and Sexting," June 2009. www.aap.org.

The American Academy of Pediatrics is an organization that represents 60,000 pediatricians.

66Burglars are now using Twitter to find victims. One Arizona man tweeted to 2,000 followers that he was heading out of town and came home to find someone had broken in and stolen thousands of dollars worth of video equipment he used for his business.**99**

—Ken and Daria Dolan, "9 Hidden Dangers of Social Networking," WalletPop, October 16, 2009. www.walletpop.com.

The Dolans are personal financial experts.

What Dangers Are Associated with Online Social Networking?

- A study published in the January 2008 issue of *Pediatrics* showed that **15 percent** of youth aged 10 to 15 had reported a **sexual solicitation** online in the past year, and 4 percent reported such an incident on a social networking site.

- Terrorism expert Gabriel Weimann states that about **90 percent of terrorist activity** on the Internet involves the use of social networking sites.

- In a survey published in April 2009 by the Center for the Digital Future, **54 percent** of parents said that online predators are a threat to the children in their households.

- According to a 2010 report by the Sophos security firm, **72 percent** of firms surveyed believe that employees' behavior on social networking sites could endanger their businesses' security.

- According to a 2008 survey by the Pew Research Center, **32 percent** of teens have experienced one or more forms of **online harassment** such as having private material forwarded without permission, receiving threatening messages, having a rumor spread about them online, or having an embarrassing photo posted online.

Parents' Main Online Concerns

A May 2009 poll commissioned by the University of Michigan's C.S. Mott Children's Hospital gauged the opinions of more than 1,000 parents in connection with safety issues and their children's use of the Internet. The top concerns for girls were online social predators and loss of privacy. The top concerns for boys were access to online pornographic material and loss of privacy.

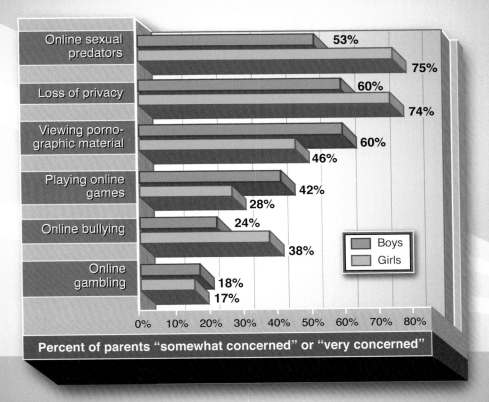

	Boys	Girls
Online sexual predators	53%	75%
Loss of privacy	60%	74%
Viewing pornographic material	60%	46%
Playing online games	42%	28%
Online bullying	24%	38%
Online gambling	18%	17%

Percent of parents "somewhat concerned" or "very concerned"

Source: C.S. Mott Children's Hospital, "Internet Predators, Privacy and Porn Concern Parents," *National Poll on Children's Health*, November 19, 2009.

- In August 2008 the Internet security company Garlik reported that nearly **25 percent** of children between the ages of 8 and 12 said they were regular users of Facebook, MySpace, or Bebo, even though this was in violation of the sites' minimum age requirements.

Facebook Perceived as Security Threat to Business

According to a survey published in January 2010 by the software security company Sophos Group, a large majority of businesses believe that Facebook presents the biggest security risk of all the social networking sites. Participants' responses are shown on this chart.

Social networks posing the biggest risk to company security

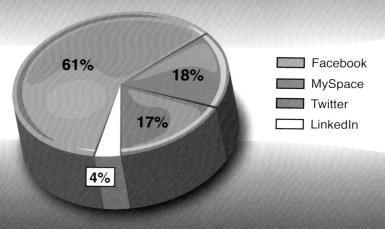

- Facebook
- MySpace
- Twitter
- LinkedIn

Source: Sophos Group, *Security Threat Report: 2010*, January 2010. www.sophos.com.

- A study published in October 2008 by researchers from the University of California–Los Angeles showed that **41 percent** of teens reported between 1 and 3 online bullying incidents over the course of a year, and **85 percent** of those teens were also bullied at school.

- A European Online Safety Survey conducted in 2009 revealed that **50 percent** of teens in Norway had been bullied online, **45 percent** in Denmark, and **29 percent** in the United Kingdom.

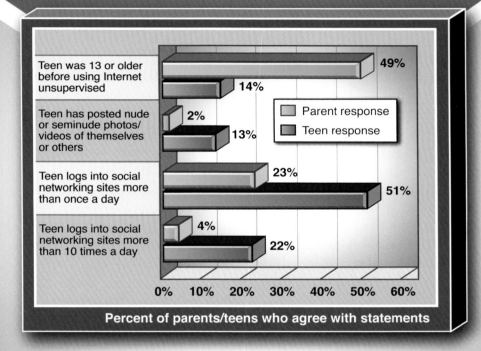

Parents Uninformed About Teens' Online Behavior

In an effort to determine how much parents really know about their kids' use of social networking sites, Common Sense Media polled adults and teenagers during May and June 2009. As this graph shows, there is a disconnect between what parents *think* their kids do online and what teenagers are actually doing.

Teen was 13 or older before using Internet unsupervised — 49% / 14%

Teen has posted nude or seminude photos/videos of themselves or others — 2% / 13%

Teen logs into social networking sites more than once a day — 23% / 51%

Teen logs into social networking sites more than 10 times a day — 4% / 22%

Parent response
Teen response

0% 10% 20% 30% 40% 50% 60%

Percent of parents/teens who agree with statements

Source: Common Sense Media, *Is Social Networking Changing Childhood? A National Poll*, August 13, 2009. www.commonsensemedia.com.

- In December 2008 a study by the National Campaign to Prevent Teen and Unplanned Pregnancy revealed that **19 percent** of participants aged 13 to 19 had sent a sexually suggestive picture or video of themselves to someone via e-mail, cell phone, or other mode, and **31 percent** had received a nude or seminude photo from someone else.

Is Online Social Networking Addictive?

66Some people become addicted to life on the computer screen, and withdraw from personal contact—it's a long way from people sitting on the porch talking to friends and neighbors.99

—Martin Baily, a senior fellow at the Brookings Institution and an adviser to the McKinsey Global Institute.

66To prove that spending too much time *online* causes social and psychological problems we compare people on how they manage *offline*. It's like comparing apples to avatars. There is a faint echo of legitimacy but once you listen closely there's nothing to hear.99

—Cory Silverberg, who is a certified sexuality educator, researcher, and author.

Tim Chai, a teenager from Carmel, Indiana, is the first to admit that he is hooked on technology. All his favorite music is loaded on his iPod, he takes his BlackBerry everywhere he goes, and he keeps up with what his friends are doing on Facebook. "I love my Internet," he says. "I love my phone. I'm not ashamed to say it."[41] Chai is so attached to his electronic gadgets that he cannot imagine even a day without them. So when he was checking out possible camps to attend during the summer of 2009, one was crossed off his list right away—because its policy stated that no cell phones or computers were allowed. Chai wanted no part of that, as he explains: "I just thought it was too much to handle."[42]

Halley Lamberson and Monica Reed, both students at San Francisco's University High School, share Chai's fondness for the Internet, especially Facebook. But they made a conscious decision to cut back drastically on their usage, as they were spending too much time online and feared they were becoming obsessed with it. Working as a two-person support group, the girls made a pact to ration their time on Facebook, allowing themselves to log in the first Saturday of each month and *only* on that day.

Their decision was applauded by Kimberly Young, who is the director of the Center for Internet Addiction Recovery in Bradford, Pennsylvania. In her work as a psychologist, Young has spoken with dozens of teenagers just like Lamberson and Reed who are trying to break the Facebook habit—and that is no easy feat for them. She explains: "It's like any other addiction. It's hard to wean yourself." Since no computer addiction programs exist specifically for teenagers, Young says that she admires young people who come up with their own strategies to reduce the amount of time they spend on social networking sites such as Facebook. "A lot of them are finding their own balance," she says. "It's like an eating disorder. You can't eliminate food. You just have to make better choices about what you eat. And what you do online."[43]

Entertainment or Obsession?

Online social networking offers a great deal of enjoyment for users, which is why it has become so popular. People can make new friends and reconnect with old, stay up to date on the latest gossip and news, keep their friends apprised of what they are doing throughout the day, and share their favorite photos and videos. One of social networking's biggest fans is J.J. Smith, a corporate executive, author, and host of the radio show *Real Talk with JJ and the Fellas*. She writes:

> I have to admit. I LOVE Facebook! I think about it when I wake up in the mornings. . . . If I happen to attend a meeting without my iPhone, I'm daydreaming about what's happening on Facebook and wondering if anyone has shared anything uplifting or funny on their wall. I have a craving and desire for Facebook with feelings similar to that of a romantic love. Facebook has created so

many new friendships in my life and has improved the overall quality of my life beyond my wildest imagination. How could I not love it? I give and receive more love to old and new friends through Facebook every day. . . . The only thing I can conclude is that I LOVE Facebook.[44]

Millions of people worldwide share Smith's fondness for Facebook and other social networking sites. As these sites offer even more features, more frills, and more opportunities to interact with friends and acquaintances, users have more incentive than ever before to spend time online.

> "
> **Those who specialize in Internet addiction often draw comparisons with other types of addictions such as alcohol, drugs, or gambling.**
> "

This may not be a problem for many of them. When it begins to take a negative toll on their health or their relationships with family and friends, however, some mental health professionals warn that they are in danger of becoming addicted. According to a Stanford University study that was published in 2008, problematic Internet use involves three criteria: the inability to cut back on Internet use or staying online longer than intended, preoccupation with the Internet when offline, and interference with personal relationships caused by excessive use.

Those who specialize in Internet addiction often draw comparisons with other types of addictions such as alcohol, drugs, or gambling. Many people who suffer from such addictions are the first to admit that their behavior is not normal, but they feel like it is out of their control and they cannot stop. The same may be said for someone who is addicted to online activity, as the Center for Internet Addiction explains:

Individuals addicted to alcohol or other drugs, for example, develop a relationship with their "chemical(s) of choice"—a relationship that takes precedence over any and all other aspects of their lives. Addicts find they need drugs merely to feel *normal*. In Internet addiction, a parallel situation exists. The Internet—like food or drugs in other addictions—provides the "high" and addicts become dependent on this cyberspace high to feel normal. . . . Internet addicts struggle to control their behaviors, and experience despair over their constant failure to do so. Their loss of self-esteem grows, fueling the need to escape even further into their addictive behaviors. A sense of powerlessness pervades the lives of addicts.[45]

The Addiction Debate

Mental health professionals often have differing views on Internet addiction, with some doubting that it exists at all. It is not currently recognized as a disorder in the American Psychiatric Association's *Diagnostic and Statistical Manual of Mental Disorders*, although there is growing support for it to be included in the revised edition due out in 2012. Those who do not accept that people can become addicted to Internet use maintain that excessive time spent online is a personal choice rather than an addiction and is not necessarily a sign of addictive behavior. As psychologist John M. Grohol explains: "Two research articles were recently published that shed more light on the so-called 'Internet addiction,' a concept we've long lampooned here due to its continuing lack of scientific validity." Grohol says virtually any behavior could be pegged as excessive, whether it is television, sex, video games, texting, Twittering, or even reading or talking to friends. He writes: "There's nothing unique or special about the Internet that suggests we should single it out for special treatment and a single diagnosis when the foundation for such a diagnosis is based upon sand. Might as well single out people's Blackberries as well."[46]

> **Mental health professionals often have differing views on Internet addiction, with some doubting that it exists at all.**

Two physicians who do not share Grohol's perspective are Dimitri A. Christakis and Megan A. Moreno. They have performed a number of studies about online social networking and online behavior, and they are convinced of the validity of Internet addiction. Their opinion is that an excessive amount of time spent online is an inevitable by-product of the electronic age. Because the Internet is such a part of modern culture, a strong potential exists for excessive use, and ultimately addiction. They write: "Part of the failure to recognize this potential 21st-century epidemic is the simple fact that many of us, Blackberry in hand, check e-mail more than we would like. The inherent difficulties in defining Internet addiction and our own need for rectification should not prevent us from recognizing an emerging epidemic."[47]

Who Is at Risk?

According to the Center for Internet Addiction, studies have found that over half of Internet addicts also have other addictions such as drugs, alcohol, smoking, and/or sex. In addition, many people who are addicted to the Internet suffer from emotional problems such as depression and anxiety-related disorders and, as the group states, "often use the fantasy world of the Internet to psychologically escape unpleasant feelings or stressful situations."[48] Following this theory, someone who suffers from addictions or mental disorders has a higher likelihood of developing an unhealthy dependence on the Internet.

> If people become so obsessed with online social networking that they cannot stand to be apart from it and it begins to consume excessive amounts of their time, this can seriously impair their relationships with family and friends.

A study published in October 2009 by researchers from Kaohsiung Medical University Hospital in Taiwan supported the belief that young people with certain mental disorders are at higher risk of developing Internet addiction. The team studied 2,293 seventh graders from 10 junior high schools in southern Taiwan to examine the relationship between Internet addiction and disorders such as attention deficit/hyperactivity disorder (ADHD), social phobia, hostility, and depression. They found that the participants who suffered from one or more of these disorders were more likely to become addicted to the Internet than youth in the general population. The most significant predictors of Internet addiction in both males and females were hostility and ADHD, while depression and social phobia predicted Internet addiction only among females. In their report, the authors write: "These results suggest that ADHD, hostility, depression and social phobia should be detected early on and intervention carried out to prevent Internet addiction in adolescents."[49]

Accompanying Problems

Some studies have shown that one of the biggest risks of Internet addiction is how it interferes with someone's ability to lead a normal, healthy life. If people become so obsessed with online social networking that they cannot stand to be apart from it and it begins to consume excessive amounts of their time, this can seriously impair their relationships with family and friends. The Center for Internet Addiction explains:

> Internet addiction has been called Internet dependency and Internet compulsivity. By any name, it is a compulsive behavior that completely dominates the addict's life. Internet addicts make the Internet a priority more important than family, friends, and work. The Internet becomes the organizing principle of addicts' lives. They are willing to sacrifice what they cherish most in order to preserve and continue their unhealthy behavior.[50]

The group adds that Internet addicts suffer from relationship problems in almost 75 percent of the cases and use interactive online applications such as chat rooms, instant messaging, or online gaming "as a safe way of establishing new relationships and more confidently relating to others through the Internet."[51]

Other side effects of Internet addiction have also been identified, one of which is its connection with self-injury. People who suffer from self-injury disorder intentionally inflict physical harm on themselves, often by cutting their skin with glass, razor blades, or other sharp objects, or by other methods such as pulling out their hair or burning themselves. A 2009 study performed by researchers from Australia examined the connection between self-harm and Internet addiction among young people. It involved 1,618 teenagers aged 13 to 18 from Guangdong Province

> The teens who were considered to be severely addicted to the Internet were nearly 5 times more likely to have self-injured in the past 6 months.

in China, 10 percent of whom were moderately addicted to the Internet and less than 1 percent of whom were severely addicted. The study showed that those who had been classified as having moderate Internet addiction were 2.4 times more likely than nonaddicted teens to have engaged in self-injurious behavior from 1 to 5 times in the past 6 months, usually by hitting, burning, or pinching themselves. The teens who were considered to be severely addicted to the Internet were nearly 5 times more likely to have self-injured in the past 6 months. From their study the researchers concluded that there was a significant correlation between Internet addiction and self-injury.

Many Questions Linger

Internet addiction, including online social networking and other computer-related activities, has been a topic of interest for a number of years. With the escalating popularity of Facebook, MySpace, Twitter, and other social networking sites, concern about addiction is growing. Mental health professionals do not always agree about whether people can become addicted to the Internet, but as researchers continue to study the issue, and more revelations are made, this may pave the way toward less speculation and more in-depth understanding.

Is Online Social Networking Addictive?

❝Research over the last decade has identified Internet addiction as a new and often unrecognized clinical disorder that impacts a user's ability to control online use to the extent that it can cause relational, occupational, and social problems.❞

—Kimberly S. Young, "Treatment Outcomes with Internet Addicts," *CyberPsychology & Behavior*, 2007. www.netaddiction.com.

Young is a psychologist who specializes in Internet addiction and online behavior and is the director of the Center for Internet Addiction Recovery.

❝I am not a firm believer of Internet Addiction. . . . People described as having Internet addiction can have problems and can suffer but this isn't due to the Internet but to other problems such as depression, anxiety and others.❞

—Walter van den Broek, "Predicting Internet Addiction or Splitting Straws?" Dr. Shock: A Neurostimulating Blog, June 18, 2008. www.shockmd.com.

Van den Broek is a psychiatrist from the Netherlands.

Bracketed quotes indicate conflicting positions.

* Editor's Note: While the definition of a primary source can be narrowly or broadly defined, for the purposes of Compact Research, a primary source consists of: 1) results of original research presented by an organization or researcher; 2) eyewitness accounts of events, personal experience, or work experience; 3) first-person editorials offering pundits' opinions; 4) government officials presenting political plans and/or policies; 5) representatives of organizations presenting testimony or policy.

❝I was so addicted to my imaginary playgroup, I put the Facebook application on my BlackBerry. That way I could know immediately when some kid who used to pick on me in elementary school was reaching out across the years to remind me that I still had cooties.❞

—Steve Tuttle, "You Can't Friend Me, I Quit!" *Newsweek*, February 4, 2009. www.newsweek.com.

Tuttle is a senior writer for *Newsweek* magazine.

❝Many teens appear to have a hard time unplugging from social networking sites for any period of time. This addictive access appears to be tied to social anxiety. . . . If teens measure their social worth based on the level of electronic communication activity with friends, this can fuel addiction.❞

—Nancy E. Willard, *Cyber-Safe Kids, Cyber-Savvy Teens*. San Francisco: Jossey-Bass, 2007.

Willard is a lawyer and educational technology consultant who often speaks about issues related to online youth risk.

❝Research and case studies are presenting considerable evidence that Internet addiction, like drug or other addictions, can have a similar debilitating impact on its subjects.❞

—Blake Bertagna, "The Internet—Disability or Distraction? An Analysis of Whether 'Internet Addiction' Can Qualify as a Disability Under the Americans with Disabilities Act," *Hofstra Labor & Employment Law Journal*, February 4, 2009. http://law.hofstra.edu.

Bertagna is an attorney in Washington, D.C.

❝All Internet use—even heavy Internet use—is not inherently bad or problematic or 'addicting.' It's a far more subtle relationship, and one that most current 'Internet addiction' measures are not accounting for.❞

—John M. Grohol, "The Internet Addiction Myth: 2009 Update," Psych Central, January 31, 2009. http://psychcentral.com.

Grohol is a psychologist and the CEO and founder of the Psych Central mental health online social networking site.

❝The study of possible internet addiction is still at a very early stage.❞

—Charles P. O'Brien, "Commentary on Tao et al. (2010): Internet Addiction and DSM-V," Wiley InterScience, February 5, 2010. www3.interscience.wiley.com.

O'Brien is a psychiatry professor at the University of Pennsylvania.

❝Medically sanctioning the category of 'behavioral addictions' also changes how we will think about freedom and responsibility. Making bad choices, developing destructive habits, and attempting solutions to problems in living that then become serious problems themselves will all become less important as the locus of responsibility shifts from the person doing something to the something being done.❞

—Todd Essig, "DSM-5 Opens the Diagnostic Door to 'Internet Addiction,'" True/Slant, February 10, 2010. http://trueslant.com.

Essig is a psychologist and psychoanalyst from New York City.

❝The Internet has become one of the most important information resources for adolescents. However, addiction to the Internet can also have a negative impact on academic performance, family relationships, and emotional state in adolescents.❞

—Chih-Hung Ko et al., "Predictive Values of Psychiatric Symptoms for Internet Addiction in Adolescents," *Archives of Pediatrics & Adolescent Medicine*, October 2009. http://archpedi.ama-assn.org.

Ko is a psychiatrist and researcher from Taiwan.

❝Internet addiction is a compulsive behavior that leads people to isolate themselves from others, put off or fail to live up to obligations and engage in potentially self destructive or illegal behaviors.❞

—Indiana University Health Center, "Internet Addiction and Gambling," 2008. www.iub.edu.

The Indiana University Health Center provides medical and psychological health services to the school's students, spouses, and dependents.

Facts and Illustrations

Is Online Social Networking Addictive?

- According to the Center for Internet Addiction Recovery, **5 to 10 percent** of Americans suffer from Internet addiction, which represents 15 million to 30 million people.

- In February 2009 researchers from Taiwan announced a study involving more than 9,000 teenagers, in which **25 percent** of males and **13 percent** of females reported that they were addicted to the Internet.

- A study published in the October 2009 issue of *Archives of Pediatrics & Adolescent Medicine* states that adolescents with depression, attention deficit/hyperactivity disorder, and/or social phobia are more likely to develop **Internet addiction** than those without the disorders.

- The Center for Internet Addiction Recovery states that **cybersex/cyberporn** addiction is the most common form of Internet addiction.

- In March 2009 researchers from Switzerland published a survey involving 94 Swiss psychiatrists who were asked for their views on Internet addiction; 20 rejected the concept and its importance, while 74 considered it to be a real **clinical problem**.

- In 2008 the *American Journal of Psychiatry* published an editorial in support of naming Internet addiction as an **official mental condition**.

- Studies have shown that more than **50 percent** of Internet addicts also suffer from other addictions such as drugs, alcohol, smoking, and sex.

Hooked on Social Networking

Some mental health professionals say the potential for addiction to online social networking is a serious problem. Although it may not be an indication that someone is addicted, a March 2010 survey by the consumer electronics company Retrevo found that respondents under age 25 frequently log into Facebook and/or Twitter during the night and early in the morning. This graph shows how participants responded when asked questions about their online habits.

Morning and night log-in habits, Facebook and/or Twitter

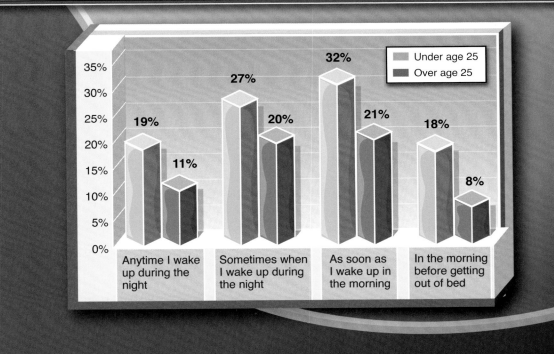

Source: Andrew Eisner, "Is Social Media a New Addiction?" Retrevo Blog, March 15, 2010. www.retrevo.com.

- According to psychiatrist Elias Aboujaoude, Internet addiction shares features in common with **substance abuse, impulse control disorder**, and **obsessive-compulsive disorder**.

Addiction Warning Signs

According to Hilarie Cash, executive director of the Internet addiction center ReSTART, there are 11 signs of Internet addiction, with 3 of the symptoms indicating abuse and 5 or more a likely sign of addiction.

11 warning signs of Internet addiction

A heightened sense of euphoria while on the Internet
Spending increased amounts of time online
Behavior change: Marked loss of control (online and/or offline)
Neglecting family and friends
Loss of interest in non-Internet-related activities
Being dishonest with others about Internet usage
Interference with school and job responsibilities
Craving more time online, restless when away from computer
Feeling guilty or ashamed about how much time is spent online
Change in sleep patterns
Adverse health symptoms such as change in weight, backaches, headaches, or carpal tunnel syndrome

Source: Boston.com, "11 Signs of Internet Addiction," September 4, 2009. www.boston.com.

- A study announced in December 2009 by researchers from Australia and China showed that teenagers who are addicted to the Internet are more likely to engage in **self-harming behaviors** such as pulling out their hair or hitting, pinching, or burning themselves.

- Survey results announced in February 2010 by researchers from China showed that as many as **15.6 percent** of Chinese Internet users aged 18 to 23 were addicted to the Internet.

- In February 2009 researchers from Taiwan reported that Internet-addicted teens are more prone to **aggressive behavior** (such as threatening or hurting others) than other adolescents.

- According to the Center for Internet Addiction Recovery, Internet addicts suffer from relationship problems in nearly **75 percent** of cases and use online chat rooms and other social networking sites to establish new relationships.

Should Online Social Networking Be More Tightly Regulated?

> ❝Many think the Internet is a good thing because it is unregulatable. The Internet is good, but not because it cannot be regulated.❞
>
> Joseph Reagle, who holds a PhD in media, culture, and communication from New York University and has written extensively about the Internet and new media.

> ❝Internet governance is a large, complex, and ambiguous topic.❞
>
> —Lawrence B. Solum, a law professor at the University of Illinois College of Law.

On April 29, 2010, Massachusetts lawmakers unanimously approved groundbreaking legislation that was signed into law by the governor five days later. The new law, which is among the toughest of its kind in the United States, makes bullying of students—including cyberbullying—illegal in the state. It prohibits any actions that could cause emotional or physical harm, including bullying at schools, on school buses, and through electronic means such as social networking sites, cell phones, and e-mail. It outlaws retaliation against anyone who reports bullying to authorities; mandates antibullying training for teachers, support staff, and students from kindergarten through twelfth grade; and requires that parents be informed of bullying incidents. Another important part of the bill is the requirement that all school employees, including custodians, people who work in cafeterias, and bus drivers, report incidents of suspected bullying, and that school administrators investigate every case.

The catalyst for the new legislation was the tragic stories of two Massachusetts students: Carl Joseph Walker-Hoover, an 11-year-old boy from Springfield, and Phoebe Prince, a 15-year-old girl from Ireland who had recently moved to New Hadley. The two did not know each other, but they shared a common experience: Both had been relentlessly bullied by classmates, and both had committed suicide by hanging themselves. Their deaths sparked public outrage and galvanized support for laws that would protect young people and prevent such tragic incidents from happening again. In praise of the new legislation, Massachusetts senator Richard R. Tisei issued this statement: "No child should ever have to endure the constant harassment that Phoebe and other young bullying victims have been subject to. My hope is that these changes we have made today will make our schools safer for all students."[52]

The Push for Tougher Laws

Massachusetts is among the 43 states that have passed laws prohibiting bullying and cyberbullying. According to the watchdog organization Bully Police, some state laws that have been enacted are not tough enough. For instance, the group ranks the antibullying legislation in Minnesota and Texas as below average and notes that Missouri has a cyberbullying clause on the books but no antibullying law. Because this legislation varies so much from state to state, a growing number of legislators, parents, and advocacy organizations support the enactment of federal laws.

One piece of legislation that has been proposed, known as the Megan Meier Cyberbullying Prevention Act, is named after a 13-year-old Missouri girl who committed suicide after being harassed on MySpace. Megan had been communicating with a person she thought was a teenage boy named Josh Evans. After being attentive and friendly toward her, his behavior abruptly changed and he

> **Massachusetts is among the 43 states that have passed laws prohibiting bullying and cyberbullying.**

sent her an e-mail message that said, "The world would be a better place without you."[53] Megan became so distraught that she hanged herself in her bedroom—and she died having no idea that Josh Evans did not exist.

> **Although the proposed Megan Meier Cyberbullying Prevention Act has many supporters, it also has numerous detractors.**

The person who had been harassing Megan was actually a 47-year-old neighbor named Lori Drew.

Drew was arrested and convicted on three counts of computer fraud, but a U.S. district judge threw out the guilty verdicts and ordered that she be acquitted. Yet even though Drew escaped punishment, the tragic case drew support for tougher cyberbullying laws, which resulted in the legislation named after Megan. If it is passed by the U.S. Congress, cyberbullying would become punishable by a fine and up to two years in prison.

U.S. Representative Linda Sanchez, who introduced the bill along with 14 other members of Congress, shares her perspective about why the law is crucial:

> We have laws criminalizing stalking, sexual harassment, identity theft and more when it takes place in person and online. All of these actions have consequences. But there is one serious online offense that has no penalty—cyberbullying. Do we not think it is as serious because it takes place in cyberspace and not face to face? . . . It's happening everywhere and it follows kids home—occurring at any hour of the day or night. Cyberbullying is hurtful enough and affecting kids enough that its victims have turned to suicide or violence just to make it stop. Should we just ignore it? Pass it off as simple child's play?[54]

Regulation Controversy

Although the proposed Megan Meier Cyberbullying Prevention Act has many supporters, it also has numerous detractors. Those who are against such legislation do not disagree that young people should feel safe while they are online and should not be subjected to harassment on social networking sites or any other electronic medium. The opponents argue, however, that implementing federal legislation is not the answer. A major reason for their objection is that this particular bill's language is vague and therefore rife with opportunities for misinterpretation. Even some child safety advocates believe the legislation is well-meaning but the wrong approach, as technology journalist and Internet safety expert Larry Magid explains: "Even if you wanted to, you can't legislate against meanness. It's contextual. If I call you fat, maybe I was bullying, or maybe I was concerned about your health, or maybe it was a relatively innocuous slight."[55]

Another person who objects to such legislation is University of California–Los Angeles law professor Eugene Volokh. He, too, argues that if the bill were passed, it could subject people to stiff punishments for posting their opinions on a social networking site or blog, calling someone with whom they disagree a derogatory name, or participating in a contentious online argument. He explains: "The bill defines it as 'using electronic means to support severe, repeated and hostile behavior,' but what does 'severe, hostile and repeated behavior' mean? I've written several articles opposing the bill that have appeared online. That's electronic and—because I've written a few of them—repeated. I was also severe and hostile in my criticisms. Under [this] law, I can now go to jail."[56]

> "Any laws that are designed to limit people's ability to talk freely online have been challenged as a violation of the U.S. Constitution's guarantee of freedom of speech."

A Constitutional Right to Free Speech

One of Volokh's main objections to the Megan Meier bill, as well as any antibullying legislation, is his belief that it is unconstitutional. His viewpoint is shared by civil rights lawyers, libertarian organizations, and plaintiffs' attorneys throughout the United States. Any laws that are designed to limit people's ability to talk freely online have been challenged as a violation of the U.S. Constitution's guarantee of freedom of speech.

In fact, as soon as the Massachusetts antibullying law had been signed by the governor, it was already a subject of contention. Evan Cohen, a lawyer from Los Angeles, explains: "The people who pass these laws want to make everything better, I understand that. They want to protect children, I understand that, too. But that doesn't mean it's constitutional."[57]

Cohen has firsthand experience with challenging a cyberbullying charge. A middle school in Beverly Hills, California, suspended his daughter in May 2008 for posting a derogatory video about another girl on the YouTube site. Cohen's daughter took the case to federal court, claiming that her First Amendment rights had been violated. U.S. district court judge Steven V. Wilson sided with her, saying that the school had indeed infringed on her right to free speech. In his opinion, the judge wrote:

> To allow the school to cast this wide a net and suspend a student simply because another student takes offense to their speech, without any evidence that such speech caused a substantial disruption of the school's activities, runs afoul of the law. The court cannot uphold school discipline of student speech simply because young persons are unpredictable or immature, or because, in general, teenagers are emotionally fragile and may often fight over hurtful comments.[58]

Facebook in the Hot Seat

With 500 million members worldwide as of June 2010, Facebook is more popular than any other social networking site. But as its popularity has grown, public attention has been drawn to its lax privacy policies, and they have been the target of sharp criticism. A major target of the criticism is Facebook's creator and chief executive, Mark Zuckerberg, who has made it clear that user privacy is not of particular concern to him. In fact, in January 2010 Zuckerberg publicly stated that if he were to create Facebook today, user information would be public by default, not private as it has been in the years since the site went online.

Zuckerberg's lackadaisical attitude about users' privacy has not been well received by many who frequent the site, including technology experts. Their concerns erupted into a firestorm of controversy in April

2010. Facebook announced changes to its privacy settings that allowed sharing of users' personal profile information with third-party Web sites, thereby usurping users' ability to restrict such access. Research analyst Avivah Litan explains why this was such a contentious issue: "Facebook advertises its privacy features as giving users the ability to control the sharing of information they post on Facebook, but the firm does not warn those users that those controls can go awry. There are no regulations protecting consumers from the malfunctioning of those controls, and there needs to be. In other words, there need to be penalties when companies don't protect their customers' private information, especially when those customers are told that they are in control of their own information."[59]

Less than a month after the changes were implemented, 15 consumer groups filed a formal complaint with the Federal Trade Commission (FTC), claiming that Facebook had violated the privacy rights of its users. In a May 5, 2010, filing titled *Complaint, Request for Investigation, Injunction, and Other Relief*, the plaintiffs state that the right to privacy is a fundamental right in the United States, and this includes the collection, use, and dissemination of personal infor-

> A major target of the criticism is Facebook's creator and chief executive, Mark Zuckerberg, who has made it clear that user privacy is not of particular concern to him.

mation by any entity. Senator Charles E. Schumer of New York, one of the people involved in the court filing, urged the FTC to issue formal guidelines for all social networking sites that would dictate how private information provided by users could be used and disseminated. In a letter to the FTC, Schumer wrote: "I am asking the FTC to use the authority given to it to examine practices in the disclosure of private information from social networking sites and to ensure users have the ability to prohibit the sharing of personal information. If the FTC feels it does not have the authority to do so under current regulations I will support them in obtaining the tools and authority to do just that."[60]

The lead group in the complaint against Facebook was the Electronic

Privacy Information Center (EPIC). In the May 5, 2010, document, EPIC details how users' privacy has been violated, saying that Facebook's privacy settings and policies "are inconsistent with the site's information sharing practices, and Facebook misleads users into believing that users can still maintain control over their personal information." The group goes on to explain how users are misled by the new privacy settings: "Facebook discloses information that users designate as available to 'Friends Only' to third party websites and applications, as well as other Facebook users, and outsiders who happen upon Facebook pages or Community Pages." EPIC strongly recommends that the FTC undertake a full investigation of Facebook, as the complaint states: "EPIC urges the Commission to investigate Facebook, determine the extent of the harm to consumer privacy and safety, require Facebook to restore privacy settings that were previously available . . . require Facebook to give users meaningful control over personal information, and seek appropriate injunctive and compensatory relief."[61]

A Complicated Issue

Because of the numerous factors involved, including privacy rights and constitutional protections, any attempt to tighten regulation of online social networking is fraught with controversy. Advocates continue to fight to make Internet laws tougher in an effort to cut down on privacy violations, online harassment, cyberbullying, and Internet crime. Those who oppose tougher legislation stress that while these issues are important and should be addressed, passing laws that limit free speech is not the answer.

Should Online Social Networking Be More Tightly Regulated?

66 When so-called free speech leads to bullies having free-reign [*sic*] to threaten kids, it is time to act. . . . The Megan Meier Cyberbullying Prevention Act would criminalize bullying like this when perpetrators hide behind the emboldening anonymity of the web. Severe online bullying must have consequences. 99

—Linda Sanchez, "Protecting Victims, Preserving Freedoms," *Huffington Post*, May 6, 2009. www.huffingtonpost.com.

Sanchez is a U.S. representative from California.

66 I believe we must usher in a new era of Internet safety education and cyber-crime awareness. Instead of preventing our children from using the Internet, or criminalizing speech online that would be permissible on the playground, we must instead teach children how to be good cyber-citizens. 99

—Debbie Wasserman Schultz, testimony before the U.S. House of Representatives Committee on the Judiciary, September 30, 2009. http://judiciary.house.gov.

Schultz is a U.S. representative from Florida.

* Editor's Note: While the definition of a primary source can be narrowly or broadly defined, for the purposes of Compact Research, a primary source consists of: 1) results of original research presented by an organization or researcher; 2) eyewitness accounts of events, personal experience, or work experience; 3) first-person editorials offering pundits' opinions; 4) government officials presenting political plans and/or policies; 5) representatives of organizations presenting testimony or policy.

66 What are Rep. Linda Sanchez and the others thinking here? Are they just taking the view that 'criminalize it all, let the prosecutors sort it out'? Even if that's
so, won't their work amount to nothing, if the law is
struck down as . . . overbroad—as I'm pretty certain
it would be? Or are they just trying to score political
points here with their constituents, with little regard
to whether the law will actually do any good? 99

—Eugene Volokh, "'Severe, Repeated, and Hostile' Speech?" Volokh Conspiracy, April 30, 2009. www.volokh.com.

Volokh is a law professor at the University of California–Los Angeles School of
Law and the founder of the Volokh Conspiracy blog.

66 Facebook's changes to users' privacy settings disclose
personal information to the public that was previously
restricted. Facebook's changes to users' privacy settings also disclose personal information to third par-
ties that was previously not available. These changes
violate user expectations, diminish user privacy, and
contradict Facebook's own representations. 99

—Electronic Privacy Information Center, *Complaint, Request for Investigation, Injunction, and Other Relief*, May 5, 2010.
http://epic.org.

The Electronic Privacy Information Center seeks to focus public attention on civil
liberties issues and to protect privacy and constitutional rights.

66 We have heard the feedback. . . . In the coming weeks,
we will add privacy controls that are much simpler
to use. We will also give you an easy way to turn off
all third-party services. We are working hard to make
these changes available as soon as possible. 99

—Mark Zuckerberg, "From Facebook, Answering Privacy Concerns with New Settings," *Washington Post*, May 24, 2010.
www.washingtonpost.com.

Zuckerberg is the founder and chief executive of Facebook.

66 A law gives schools the power to do something about a bullying problem. Without a law, school districts may choose not to create anti-bullying policies, or may not actually enforce policies. 99

—Anti-Defamation League, *Bullying/Cyberbullying Prevention Law*, April 2009. www.adl.org.

The Anti-Defamation League fights bigotry in the United States and abroad through information, education, legislation, and advocacy.

66 Not only is cyber bullying a most venal and intolerable abuse of the freedom of speech that Internet users enjoy but, because of new and vastly different technologies, cyber bullying has eluded sanctions that protect potential victims of more traditional abuses such as stalking, threats and the like. And because of the interstate nature of such abuses, new federal legislation is critically needed. 99

—Robert M. O'Neil, testimony before the U.S. House of Representatives Committee on the Judiciary, September 30, 2009. http://judiciary.house.gov.

O'Neil is director of the Thomas Jefferson Center for the Protection of Free Expression in Charlottesville, Virginia.

66 New legislation could help to address cyberbullying and other online safety problems. But newly criminalizing a broad swath of online speech is not the right general approach. Nor do I favor a set of rules that apply only in cyberspace and not in offline life. 99

—John Palfrey, testimony before the U.S. House of Representatives Committee on the Judiciary, September 30, 2009. http://judiciary.house.gov.

Palfrey is a professor of law and vice dean for library and information resources at Harvard Law School.

Should Online Social Networking Be More Tightly Regulated?

- As of 2009, 37 U.S. states had adopted legislation mandating that schools implement **antibullying statutes**.

- Legislation known as the Deleting Online Predators Act, which would have **banned the use of online social networking sites in schools and libraries** that receive federal technology funding, was passed by the House of Representatives in 2006 but died in the Senate.

- In 2009 U.S. representative Linda Sanchez introduced legislation that would make it a **federal crime** punishable by up to two years in prison for electronic speech that harasses, intimidates, or causes substantial emotional distress to a person.

- According to a Rasmussen poll published in June 2008, **73 percent** of respondents believe it should be a crime to harass someone on the Internet, and **13 percent** believe it should not be a crime.

- A Rasmussen poll published in June 2008 showed that stronger federal regulation of the Internet was favored by **55 percent** of female respondents and **46 percent** of male respondents.

- A 2008 study of 1,000 British people showed that 9 out of 10 favor **tighter governmental regulation** of online social networking sites.

Legislating Against Bullying

Forty-three U.S. states* have enacted legislation that prohibits student bullying with some of the laws also prohibiting cyberbullying. This table shows the states that have such legislation in place and the year it went into effect.

1999	2000	2001	2002
Georgia	New Hampshire	Colorado, Louisiana, Mississippi, Oregon, West Virginia	Connecticut, New Jersey, Oklahoma, Washington
2003	**2004**	**2005**	**2006**
Arkansas, California, Rhode Island	Vermont	Arizona, Indiana, Maryland, Virginia, Texas, Tennessee, Maine, Nevada	Idaho, South Carolina, Alaska, New Mexico
2007	**2008**	**2009**	**2010**
Delaware, Iowa, Illinois, Kansas, Minnesota, Ohio, Pennsylvania	Nebraska, Kentucky, Utah, Florida	North Carolina, Wyoming, Alabama	Massachusetts, Wisconsin

*Note: Missouri has a cyberbullying clause but no antibullying legislation.

Source: Bully Police USA, "Anti Bullying Law Passage Calender," 2010. www.bullypolice.org.

- Under U.S. law, officials from Facebook, MySpace, and other Web sites are prohibited from turning over user content without a **search warrant** that is issued based on probable cause.

Dwindling Support for Government Regulation

In April 2010, the electronic media company Rasmussen Reports conducted a national survey of 1,000 American adults to find out their opinions about Internet regulation by the government. As these charts show, support for tighter regulation has decreased substantially since a survey conducted by the same group in 2008.

Should the Federal Communications Commission regulate the Internet like it does radio and television?

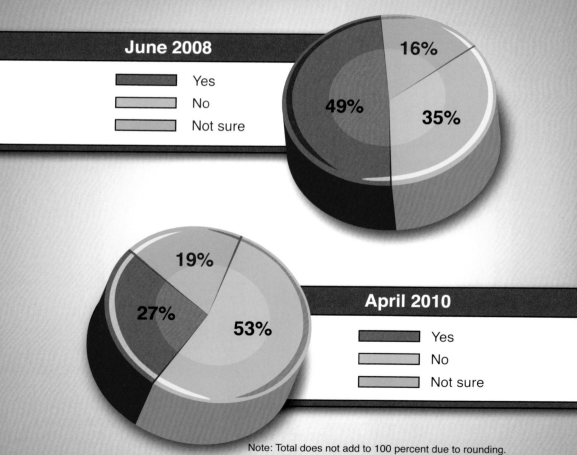

June 2008

- Yes
- No
- Not sure

16%

49%

35%

19%

27%

53%

April 2010

- Yes
- No
- Not sure

Note: Total does not add to 100 percent due to rounding.

Sources: Rasmussen Reports, "49% Say Government Should Regulate Internet," June 21, 2008; Rasmussen Reports, "53% Oppose FCC Regulation of the Internet," April 9, 2010. www.rasmussenreports.com.

Sexting Legislation

Sexting is the sharing of nude or sexually explicit photographs and/or videos via cell phone text messages, online social networking sites, or e-mail. Despite the risks involved, the practice is becoming more common among teens. As of May 2010, 15 U.S. states had introduced legislation that aims to educate young people about the risks of sexting, deter them from taking part in it, and apply appropriate penalties to those who do engage in sexting. Some states, even several that have not enacted legislation, have clamped down on sexting by charging people who engage in it with possession and/or distribution of child pornography.

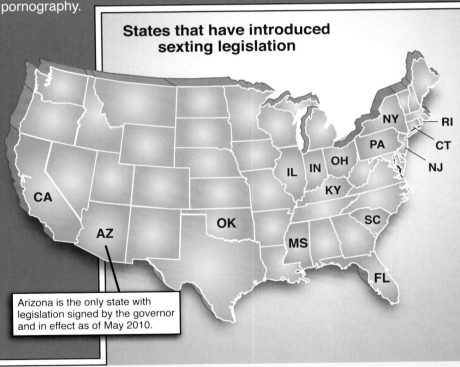

States that have introduced sexting legislation

Arizona is the only state with legislation signed by the governor and in effect as of May 2010.

Source: National Conference of State Legislatures, "2009 'Sexting' Legislation," February 22, 2010. www.ncsl.org.

- In 2008 MySpace and Facebook entered into agreements with the attorneys general of 49 states and the District of Columbia to provide better protection of children from **online predators** and inappropriate content.

Key People and Advocacy Groups

Parry Aftab: A well-known Internet security expert and activist on behalf of protecting young people from the dangers of cyberspace.

Tim Berners-Lee: The developer of Web software and the first point-and-click browser, who is considered the father of the World Wide Web.

danah boyd: A researcher at Microsoft Research and a fellow at Harvard's Berkman Center for Internet and Society who has written extensively on the topic of online social networking.

Center for Democracy and Technology: A civil liberties group that works to keep the Internet open and available to all.

Common Sense Media: An organization that provides information on media and entertainment content to the public.

Electronic Frontier Foundation: A civil liberties organization that advocates on behalf of the public interest with regard to Internet-related issues such as free speech, privacy, innovation, and consumer rights.

Electronic Privacy Information Center: A public interest research center that seeks to focus public attention on civil liberties issues and to protect privacy, the First Amendment, and constitutional rights.

John M. Grohol: A psychologist who founded the Psych Central mental health online social networking site.

Internet Education Foundation: A group that is dedicated to educating the public and policy makers about critical Internet-related issues.

Larry Magid: A technology journalist, Internet safety advocate, and the founder of the Web site SafeKids.

Megan Meier: A 13-year-old Missouri girl who committed suicide after being repeatedly bullied online by a woman posing as a teenage boy; her death led to a proposed cyberbullying law named after her.

Linda Sanchez: A U.S. representative from California who introduced legislation that would make it a federal crime to engage in electronic speech that harasses, intimidates, or causes substantial emotional distress to a person.

Debbie Wasserman Schultz: A U.S. representative from Florida who introduced the Adolescent Web Awareness Requires Education Act, which seeks to prevent and reduce cyberbullying through research and education, rather than making it a criminal offense.

WiredSafety: A group that provides help, information, and education with the goal of making the Internet safer for everyone.

Kimberly Young: The director of the Center for Internet Addiction Recovery and a noted authority on the subject of Internet addiction and online behavior.

Chronology

1960
Joseph C.R. Licklider, a professor at the Massachusetts Institute of Technology, describes his vision for a worldwide computer network.

1969
The first test of ARPANET (Advanced Research Projects Agency Network) is successful, proving that computers can be linked together to communicate with each other, thus launching a rudimentary version of the Internet.

1991
Swiss computer expert Tim Berners-Lee announces his creation of software and a point-and-click browser, thus launching the World Wide Web.

1995
Classmates.com goes online and allows users to seek out and communicate with friends and acquaintances from the past.

1960   1970   1980   1990

1979
Duke University students Tom Truscott and Jim Ellis, along with University of North Carolina student Steve Bellovin, launch a program they call Usenet, which allows people to post on discussion forums (known as articles) to discuss various topics of interest.

1993
Awareness of the Web spreads throughout the world: There are 130 Web sites, and the number continues to double every three months.

1994
Mosaic Communications launches the Mosaic Web browser; the company's name is later changed to Netscape Communications, and the browser is renamed Netscape Navigator.

1985
A dial-up bulletin board system known as the Whole Earth 'Lectronic Link (WELL) is launched and becomes a popular online discussion forum.

2005
The video-sharing Web site YouTube goes online and allows users to upload, share, and view videos.

2003
MySpace is launched, primarily to compete with Friendster.

1997
The Web site SixDegrees is launched; it combines the features of users being able to create and post profiles and lists of friends that are visible to others.

2010
Massachusetts and Wisconsin become the forty-second and forty-third U.S. states to pass anti-bullying legislation applicable to schools.

2006
American software architect Jack Dorsey posts "just setting up my twttr" online, thus launching the social networking/microblogging service known as Twitter, with brief posts known as "tweets."

1995   2000   2005   2010

2002
The social networking site Friendster is launched, and its popularity rapidly begins to soar.

2004
The social networking site Facebook is launched; initially it is open only to Harvard University students, but within one year it is accessible to everyone over the age of 13.

2008
MySpace and Facebook announce separate agreements with the attorneys general of 49 states and the District of Columbia that are aimed at better protecting children from online predators and inappropriate content.

2009
U.S. representative Linda Sanchez introduces the Megan Meier Cyberbullying Prevention Act, which would make electronic speech that harasses, intimidates, or causes substantial emotional distress to a person a federal crime.

Related Organizations

Center for Democracy and Technology (CDT)

1634 I St. NW, Suite 1100

Washington, DC 20006

phone: (202) 637-9800 • fax: (202) 637-0968

Web site: www.cdt.org

The CDT is a civil liberties group that works to keep the Internet open and available to all. Its Web site features news articles; information on issues such as free expression, online child safety, and Internet neutrality; press releases and statements; and a link to the CDT's blog.

Center for Internet Addiction Recovery

PO Box 72

Bradford, PA 16701

phone: (814) 451-2405 • fax: (814) 368-9560

Web site: www.netaddiction.com

The Center for Internet Addiction Recovery offers counseling for individuals, couples, and families for problematic Internet use and related issues. Its Web site offers numerous articles; frequently asked questions; information sheets on issues such as compulsive Web surfing, online gambling, and cybersex/cyberporn; statistics; and a link to the Recovery blog.

Common Sense Media

650 Townsend St., Suite 375

San Francisco, CA 94103

phone: (415) 863-0600 • fax: (415) 863-0601

e-mail: info@commonsensemedia.org

Web site: www.commonsensemedia.org

Common Sense Media is an organization that provides trustworthy information on media and entertainment content to the public. Its Web site features articles about online social networking, Internet safety, educational issues, advice for parents and educators, and a ratings section that reviews Web sites, movies, games, music, and books.

ConnectSafely

Web site: www.connectsafely.org

ConnectSafely is an interactive online-only resource for parents, teens, educators, and others who are interested in Internet safety. It offers fact sheets, press releases, safety tips, "News & Views," guest commentaries, news articles, an online forum, and a video library.

Electronic Frontier Foundation (EFF)

454 Shotwell St.

San Francisco, CA 94110-1914

phone: (415) 436-9333 • fax: (415) 436-999

e-mail: information@eff.org • Web site: www.eff.org

The EFF is a civil liberties organization that advocates on behalf of the public interest with regard to Internet-related issues such as free speech, privacy, innovation, and consumer rights. Its Web site offers news releases, current projects, annual reports, significant court victories, and the Deeplinks blog.

Electronic Privacy Information Center (EPIC)

1718 Connecticut Ave. NW, Suite 200

Washington, DC 20009

phone: (202) 483-1140 • fax: (202) 483-1248

Web site: http://epic.org

EPIC is a public interest research center that seeks to focus public attention on civil liberties issues and to protect privacy, the First Amendment, and other constitutional rights. Its Web site offers a "Hot Policy Issues" section, archived news articles, reports, and an extensive "A to Z's of Privacy" list that offers information about privacy-related issues.

Family Online Safety Institute (FOSI)

624 Ninth St. NW, Suite 222

Washington, DC 20001

phone: (202) 572-6252

e-mail: fosi@fosi.org • Web site: http://fosi.org

The FOSI seeks to make the online world safer for kids and their families by development of public policy, technology, education, and special events. Its Web site features press releases, archived news articles, safety publications for kids and parents, reports on issues such as cyberbullying and sexting, and the *Insight* newsletter.

International Network Against Cyberhate (INACH)

Camperstraat 3 hs—1091 AD

Amsterdam—The Netherlands

phone: 31-20-6927266 • fax: 31-20-6927267

e-mail: secretariat@inach.net • Web site: www.inach.net

INACH's mission is to promote respect, responsibility, and citizenship on the Internet through countering cyberhate and raising awareness about online discrimination. Its Web site features reports by INACH and its members, archived news releases, legislation, and video clips.

Internet Education Foundation (IEF)

1634 I St. NW, Suite 1100

Washington, DC 20006

phone: (202) 638-4370 • fax: (202) 637-0968

e-mail: tim@neted.org • Web site: www.neted.org

The IEF is dedicated to educating the public and policy makers about critical Internet-related issues. Although its Web site offers little more than current news articles, it links to the GetNetWise site, which features a wide variety of Internet-related publications.

National Cyber Security Alliance (NCSA)

1010 Vermont Ave. NW, Suite 821

Washington, DC 20005

phone: (202) 756-2278

e-mail: info@staysafeonline.org • Web site: www.staysafeonline.org

The NCSA's mission is to empower and support people to use the Internet securely and safely in order to protect themselves and the cyberinfrastructure. Its Web site offers a wide variety of information, including security and safety reports, studies, surveys, fact sheets, a "Safe and Secure Practices" section, news releases and alerts, and the Second Nature blog.

WiredSafety

c/o IMPS

1 Bridge St., Suite 56

Irvington-on-Hudson, NY 10533

e-mail: info@wiredsafety.org • Web site: www.wiredsafety.org

WiredSafety offers a vast amount of information about issues such as cybercrime, sexting, cyberstalking and harassment, Internet predators, and cyberdating. The site also links to WiredSafety's Teenangels, Tweenangels, WiredKids, CyberLawEnforcement, and StopCyberbullying sites.

For Further Research

Books

Ana M. Martínez Alemán and Katherine Lynk Wartman, *Online Social Networking on Campus: Understanding What Matters in Student Culture*. New York: Routledge, 2009.

Mizuko Ito, Sonja Baumer, Matteo Bittanti, and danah boyd, *Hanging Out, Messing Around, and Geeking Out: Kids Living and Learning with New Media*. Cambridge, MA: MIT, 2010.

Todd Kelsey, *Social Networking Spaces: From Facebook to Twitter and Everything In Between*. New York: Apress, 2010.

Carla Mooney, *Online Social Networking*. Detroit: Lucent, 2009.

Janella Randazza, *Go Tweet Yourself: 365 Reasons Why Twitter, Facebook, MySpace, and Other Social Networking Sites Suck*. Avon, MA: Adams, 2009.

Corey Sandler, *Living with the Internet and Online Dangers*. Teen's Guides. New York: Facts On File, 2010.

S. Craig Watkins, *The Young and the Digital: What the Migration to Social Network Sites, Games, and Anytime, Anywhere Media Means for Our Future*. Boston: Beacon, 2009.

Deanna Zandt, *Share This! How You Will Change the World with Social Networking*. San Francisco: Berrett-Koehler, 2010.

Periodicals

Anthony Bruno, "Model Makeover: As MySpace Sharpens Its Focus on Entertainment, Music Shows the Way Forward," *Billboard*, October 31, 2009.

Katie Hafner, "Driven to Distraction, Some Teens Unfriend Facebook," *Seattle Times*, December 21, 2009.

Kim Hart, "A Flashy Facebook Page, at a Cost to Privacy," *Washington Post*, June 12, 2008.

Information Week, "Social Networks Leak Personal Information," August 24, 2009.

Ashley Jones, "Let's Give Them Something to Talk About," *EContent*, March 2008.

Victoria Kim, "For Students, a Right to Be Mean Online?" *Los Angeles Times*, December 13, 2009.

Kathiann M. Kowalski, "Friend Me," *Current Health 2*, a *Weekly Reader* Publication, March 2010.

PC, "The Fragility of Social Networking," April 28, 2008.

Elaine Sciolino and Souad Mekhennet, "Al Qaeda Warrior Uses Internet to Rally Women," *New York Times*, May 28, 2008.

Dan Tynan, "The Etiquette of Social Networking: How to Make Friends Online Without Alienating Anybody," *Macworld*, October 2008.

Christina Wood, "Network Your Way into College: Can It Help You Get In?" *Careers & Colleges*, Spring 2008.

Sophia Yan, "How to Disappear from Facebook and Twitter," *Time*, January 19, 2010.

Internet Sources

Denise Caruso, "Why Is Facebook So Addictive?" *Salon*, August 7, 2008. www.salon.com/technology/machinist/blog/2008/08/07/facebook/index.html.

Tony Castro, "Valley Gangs Leave Trail on Web," *Los Angeles Daily News*, December 5, 2009. www.dailynews.com/news/ci_13931149.

Kate Dailey, "Friends with Benefits: Do Facebook Friends Provide the Same Support as Those in Real Life?" *Newsweek* blog, June 15, 2009. http://blog.newsweek.com/blogs/thehumancondition/archive/2009/06/15/friends-with-benefits-do-facebook-friends-provide-the-same-support-as-those-in-real-life.aspx.

Debra Ronca, "Are Social Networking Sites Addictive?" How Stuff Works, 2009. http://computer.howstuffworks.com/internet/social-networking/information/social-networking-sites-addictive.htm.

Social Networking, "What Is Social Networking?" 2009. www.whatissocialnetworking.com.

Source Notes

Overview

1. Quoted in danah boyd, *Why Youth ♥ Social Network Sites: The Role of Networked Publics in Teenage Social Life*, MIT Press Journals, 2008. www.mitpressjournals.org.
2. Quoted in boyd, *Why Youth ♥ Social Network Sites.*
3. Social Networking, "What Is Social Networking?" 2009. www.whatissocialnetworking.com.
4. Aric Sigman, *Well Connected? The Biological Implications of "Social Networking,"* February 2009. www.aricsigman.com.
5. boyd, *Why Youth ♥ Social Network Sites.*
6. Amanda Lenhart, *Pew Internet Project Data Memo*, January 14, 2009. www.pewinternet.org.
7. Dave Roos, "How Online Social Networks Work," How Stuff Works, August 29, 2007. http://communication.howstuffworks.com.
8. Quoted in Bill Brenner, "Slapped in the Facebook: Social Networking Dangers Exposed," *NetworkWorld*, February 9, 2009. www.networkworld.com.
9. Gabriel Weimann, "Terrorism's New Avatars—Part II," *YaleGlobal Online*, January 12, 2010. http://yaleglobal.yale.edu.
10. Quoted in Dennis Romero, "The Gangs of New Media: Criminals Get Social Too," *LA Weekly* blog, November 20, 2009. http://blogs.laweekly.com.
11. Quoted in *Calhoun Times*, "Gang Members Use Social Network Sites to Trade Info," February 2, 2010. www.calhountimes.com.
12. Internet Safety Technical Task Force, *Enhancing Child Safety & Online Technologies*, Berkman Center for Internet and Society, December 31, 2008. http://cyber.law.harvard.edu.
13. Quoted in Stuart Wolpert, "Bullying of Teenagers Online Is Common, UCLA Psychologists Report," *UCLA News*, October 2, 2008. www.newsroom.ucla.edu.
14. Quoted in Manuel Baigorri, "Internet Addiction May Be One Click Away," *Medill Reports—Washington*, July 29, 2008. http://news.medill.northwestern.edu.
15. Facebook, "Statement of Rights and Responsibilities," December 21, 2009. www.facebook.com.

How Does Online Social Networking Affect Human Interaction?

16. Sara Samuel, "The Incredible, but Not Quite Edible, Facebook!" *Radical Parenting*, April 27, 2010. www.radicalparenting.com.
17. Samuel, "The Incredible, but Not Quite Edible, Facebook!"
18. Samuel, "The Incredible, but Not Quite Edible, Facebook!"
19. Daniel Nations, "What Is Web 2.0?" About.com: Web Trends, 2010. http://webtrends.about.com.
20. Nations, "What Is Web 2.0?"
21. Nations, "What Is Web 2.0?"
22. Sigman, *Well Connected? The Biological Implications of "Social Networking."*
23. Quoted in Sharon Jayson, "'Flocking' Behavior Lands on Social Networking Sites," *USA Today*, September 28, 2009. www.usatoday.com.
24. Quoted in Jayson, "'Flocking' Behavior Lands on Social Networking Sites."
25. Mizuko Ito, Heather Horst, Matteo

Bittanti, danah boyd, Becky Herr-Stephenson, Patricia G. Lange, C.J. Pascoe, and Laura Robinson, *Living and Learning with New Media: Summary of Findings from the Digital Youth Project*, Digital Youth, November 2008. http://digitalyouth.ischool.berkeley.edu.

26. Lauren, "Lauren's Story—the Life I Almost Didn't Have," Starlight Children's Foundation. www.starlight.org.

27. Lauren, "Lauren's Story—the Life I Almost Didn't Have."

28. Quoted in Deirdre Cox Baker, "Facebook to the Rescue," *Quad-City Times*, January 8, 2010. http://qctimes.com.

What Dangers Are Associated with Online Social Networking?

29. MJD, "On the Patriots Cheerleader with the Naughty Marker," Yahoo! Sports Shutdown Corner blog, November 6, 2008. http://sports.yahoo.com.

30. Sophos, *Security Threat Report: 2010*, January 2010. www.sophos.com.

31. Go Banking Rates, "How Social Networking Puts Your Identity at Risk," February 1, 2010. www.gobankingrates.com.

32. Go Banking Rates, "How Social Networking Puts Your Identity at Risk."

33. National Center for Missing and Exploited Children, "What Is Sexting? Why Is It a Problem? What Parents and Teens Need to Know," September 21, 2009. www.missingkids.com.

34. Quoted in Patricia Reaney, "Cyberbullying, More than Just 'Messing Around,'" *Vancouver Sun*, May 12, 2009. www.vancouversun.com.

35. Wolpert, "Bullying of Teenagers Online Is Common, UCLA Psychologists Report."

36. Quoted in Cindy Kranz, "Nude Photo Led to Suicide," Cincinnati.com, March 22, 2009. http://news.cincinnati.com.

37. Quoted in Kranz, "Nude Photo Led to Suicide."

38. Quoted in Sheree Paolello, "Mom Loses Daughter over 'Sexting,' Demands Accountability," WLWT News 5, March 5, 2009. www.wlwt.com.

39. Quoted in Julie Steenhuysen, "Study Rejects Internet Sex Predator Stereotype," Reuters, February 18, 2008. www.reuters.com.

40. Quoted in Rob Cole, "Rapist Gets Life for Facebook Sex Murder," Sky News, March 8, 2010. http://news.sky.com.

Is Online Social Networking Addictive?

41. Quoted in Megan K. Scott, "Teens Panic as They're Forced to Unplug at Camp," *Houston Chronicle*, May 14, 2009. www.chron.com.

42. Quoted in Scott, "Teens Panic as They're Forced to Unplug at Camp."

43. Quoted in Katie Hafner, "To Deal with Obsession, Some Defriend Facebook," *New York Times*, December 20, 2009. www.nytimes.com.

44. J.J. Smith, "Why I Love Facebook," *Black Star News*, September 18, 2009. www.blackstarnews.com.

45. Center for Internet Addiction, "FAQs," August 15, 2009. www.netaddiction.com.

46. John M. Grohol, "The Internet Addiction Myth: 2009 Update," Psych Central, January 31, 2009. http://psychcentral.com.

47. Dimitri A. Christakis and Megan A. Moreno, "Trapped in the Net: Will Internet Addiction Become a 21st-Century Epidemic?" *Archives of Pediatric & Adolescent Medicine*, October 2009, p. 959.

48. Center for Internet Addiction, "FAQs."

49. Chih-Hung Ko, Ju-Yu Yen, Cheng-Sheng Chen, Yi-Chun Yeh, and Cheng-Fang Yen, "Predictive Values of Psychiatric Symptoms for Internet Addiction in Adolescents," *Archives of Pediatric & Adolescent Medicine*, October 2009. http://archpedi.ama-assn.org.

50. Center for Internet Addiction, "FAQs."

51. Center for Internet Addiction, "FAQs."

Should Online Social Networking Be More Tightly Regulated?

52. Quoted in Peter Schworm, "State Bill Targeting Bullying Approved," *Boston Globe*, April 30, 2010. www.boston.com.

53. Quoted in Christopher Maag, "A Hoax Turned Fatal Draws Anger but No Charges," *New York Times*, November 28, 2007. www.nytimes.com.

54. Linda Sanchez, "Protecting Victims, Preserving Freedoms," *Huffington Post*, May 6, 2009. www.huffington post.com.

55. Quoted in Steven Kotler, "Cyberbullying Bill Could Ensnare Free Speech Rights," Fox News, May 14, 2009. www.foxnews.com.

56. Quoted in Kotler, "Cyberbullying Bill Could Ensnare Free Speech Rights."

57. Quoted in Jonathan Saltzman, "Antibully Law May Face Free Speech Challenges," *Boston Globe*, May 4, 2010. www.boston.com.

58. Quoted in Victoria Kim, "For Students, a Right to Be Mean Online?" *Los Angeles Times*, December 13, 2009. http://articles.latimes.com.

59. Quoted in Brian Prince, "Do Facebook Privacy Concerns Really Require Government Regulation?" eWeek, May 6, 2010. www.eweek.com.

60. Charles E. Schumer, "Decision by Facebook to Share Users' Private Information with Third-Party Websites Raises Privacy Concerns," April 26, 2010. http://schumer.senate.gov.

61. Electronic Privacy Information Center, *Complaint, Request for Investigation, Injunction, and Other Relief, Before the Federal Trade Commission*, Washington, DC, May 5, 2010. http://epic.org.

List of Illustrations

Index

Note: Boldface page numbers refer to illustrations.

About the Author

Peggy J. Parks holds a bachelor of science degree from Aquinas College in Grand Rapids, Michigan, where she graduated magna cum laude. She has written more than 90 nonfiction educational books for children and young adults. Parks lives in Muskegon, Michigan, a town that she says inspires her writing because of its location on the shores of Lake Michigan.